MW00603345

SECRET

HILL COUNTRY

A Guide to the Weird, Wonderful, and Obscure

Cheryl and Les Thomas

Copyright © 2022, Reedy Press, LLC
All rights reserved.

Reedy Press
PO Box 5131
St. Louis, MO 63139
www.reedypress.com

No part of this publication may be reproduced or transmitted in any form or by any means, electronic or mechanical, including photocopy, recording, or any information storage and retrieval system, without permission in writing from the publisher. Permissions may be sought directly from Reedy Press at the above mailing address or via our website at www.reedypress.com.

Library of Congress Control Number: 2021935134
ISBN: 9781681063331

Design by Jill Halpin

Unless otherwise indicated, all photos are courtesy of the author or in the public domain.

We (the publisher and the author) have done our best to provide the most accurate information available when this book was completed. However, we make no warranty, guarantee, or promise about the accuracy, completeness, or currency of the information provided, and we expressly disclaim all warranties, express or implied. Please note that attractions, company names, addresses, websites, and phone numbers are subject to change or closure, and this is outside of our control. We are not responsible for any loss, damage, injury, or inconvenience that may occur due to the use of this book. When exploring new destinations, please do your homework before you go. You are responsible for your own safety and health when using this book.

Printed in the United States of America
22 23 24 25 26   5 4 3 2 1

For Margo and Dan, and Joy and Bob

CONTENTS

INTRODUCTION

In the Hill Country, west of Austin and San Antonio, winding roads stretch out for more than 100 miles over hills as rugged and rawboned as the hide on a longhorn steer. Springtime turns them into garden paths, lined with wildflowers. Some of them lead to adventures that are purely magical. Top a hill and catch a vision of a lofty German castle rising out of the greenery of live oaks and ash junipers that Texans call cedars. Or feast your eyes on unspoiled scenery that rolls on for miles, without a house in sight.

Each season turns another page of beauty. At harvest time, in vineyards that lace the valleys, vines bend under loads of ripening grapes. In San Saba, where *Lonesome Dove* star Tommy Lee Jones rides the range in real life, pecans rain from lofty trees on rural roads. It's the pecan capital of the world.

The Hill Country is filled with hidden, secret treasures. Jim Bowie never found his lost silver mine, but a blind man discovered a mountain of granite, enough to build the state capitol and half the country's skyscrapers. Along the way, he led a cattle drive, and built a town. Where can you find a haunted saloon? Whatever happened to Ralph the Swimming pig? Why does a town only have one parking meter? Why are the fleas in a museum wearing clothes?

Need a cooking spoon to measure a "smidgeon," or a bottle of bluebonnet perfume? Find those forgotten gems in towns with sturdy homes and shops crafted by German pioneers nearly two centuries ago. Go where country lanes chase after spring-fed rivers, clear as liquid glass, splashing over rocks—a happy sound. You could swear it sounds like laughter. Sunset comes. Listen to the music of a lonesome country song spilling out into the night. Watch a couple dancing under the stars. Bob Wills traveled these roads, one dancehall at a time. So did Elvis, and Lyndon Johnson, and hardy German pioneers, and roaming bands of Comanche horsemen, moving silently under a full moon. In the wildness of the hills, reaching across 31,000 square miles, you almost believe you could catch up with them, just around the bend. Come along and see it for yourself.

SWEET SCENT

How do you translate the bluebonnet from the roadside to the perfume bottle?

Bluebonnets are as important to Texas as tulips are to Holland. They raise their heads in the springtime and cover fields and roadsides. Totally recognizable for their bonnet shape and purplish blue color, they gained fame during Lady Bird Johnson's years as First Lady. She used this humble wildflower and others to beautify barren roadsides. However, they have a longer life when blended with oils by an accomplished herbal chemist and parfumier. Travel to Fredericksburg and you'll meet one.

Urban Herbal in Fredericksburg is the home of a small local laboratory that produces organic colognes and edible flower products such as vinegars and salts. The man behind the creative reimagining of natural herbs and flowers is Bill Varney, a lifelong horticulturist. He's never been afraid to try something different such as his year in Tasmania, Australia, working in agriculture. He eventually returned to the Hill Country to open Fredericksburg Herb Farm. After more than two decades, the Varneys sold the herb farm and downsized to Urban Herbal with its smaller footprint but same dedication to using indigenous herbs and flowers to create the beautiful landscape complete with a labyrinth and a meditation garden for quiet moments.

BOUNTIFUL HARVEST

WHAT: Urban Herbal

WHERE: 407 Whitney St., Fredericksburg, TX

WHEN: Tuesday through Saturday, 10 a.m. to 5 p.m.

COST: Bluebonnet cologne $20 to $35

PRO TIP: Watch where you walk in the gardens. You might meet up with a squirrel or a friendly spider. Take time to look at the artwork of featured local artists.

Top: *Bill Varney, a lifelong horticulturist in Fredericksburg, grows native Hill Country plants at Urban Herbal.*

Left inset: *Varney produces edible flower products and organic colognes, including a fragrance made from bluebonnets.*

Right inset: *Varney crafts perfume from bluebonnets.*

Varney is intent upon using only natural ingredients in colognes, toiletries, and vinegars. He noted that people who complain about being put off by commercial fragrances find the farm's scents to be pleasing and wearable. Using his knowledge of natural scents of flowers and herbs, he found a way to blend them to create a scent for an icon that is not known for its smell. The bluebonnet cologne blends the fragrances of lilacs and hyacinths and lilies of the valley along with an added note of vanilla.

Visit Urban Herbal garden to discover how herbs and flowers come together organically to create toiletries as well as natural vinegars. If you're very lucky, you might get to enjoy a private dinner cooked by Bill Varney and served in the farm's large greenhouse, complete with an elegant chandelier and assorted visitors such as butterflies and a friendly garden spider or two.

Urban Herbal brings the beauty of the garden to the dressing table as well as the dining table.

SPIRITS HAUNT THE BACKBONE TAVERN

Where can you spend a happy hour at a haunted tavern?

They call it the Devil's Backbone Tavern, but not everyone who hangs around here has a spine. Perched beside the high road that twists between San Marcos and Blanco, the "Backbone" is known for the ghosts that haunt it. Unexplained oddities run the gamut from flickering lights and furniture that mysteriously changes positions to a stone in the center of the fireplace that many swear looks like a devilish profile.

On the spine of the ridge known as the Devil's Backbone that runs nearby, some swear they've seen squads of ghostly Confederate horsemen race by. A woman carrying a child and calling out for her husband is another apparition who haunts the neighborhood. There have been enough spooky sightings to fill an episode of *Unsolved Mysteries*. In fact, one aired on February 22, 2017, that was filmed around the Backbone.

Inside the rock fronted tavern, opened in 1936, regulars fill the stools that line the long bar. There's a weathered shuffleboard that stays in constant use. Dollar bills, signed by patrons, paper the ceiling. *Texas Monthly* named it one of the best honky tonks in Texas and called the regulars "bibulous."

"We didn't know what that meant," a bartender says. "We had to look it up. It said someone who likes to drink. We said, 'yeah, that's us.' Now we hold a Bibulous Birthday Party on the 15th of every month for everyone who has a birthday that month."

Do the regulars at this tavern include a gang of ghosts, or are they just bibulous pranksters?

HIGH SPIRITS

WHAT: Devil's Backbone Tavern

WHERE: 4041 FM 32, Fischer, TX; devilsbackbonetavern.com; (830) 964-2544

COST: Beer starts at $2.50

PRO TIP: Punch 0-4-0-9 on the juke box and you can hear Todd Snider sing "The Ballad of the Devil's Backbone Tavern," a song he wrote after getting lost on his way to another gig and winding up at the Backbone. It's also available on YouTube.

Top: *Beneath the ceiling papered with money, lively spirits sometimes appear at the tavern.*

Bottom: *The roadside tavern is a landmark on the twisted road known as the Devil's Backbone.*

Musicians also take the stage regularly. The Backbone's owners are musicians themselves. Singer-songwriter Robyn Ludwick, her husband John, aka Lunch Meat, and their partner Abbey Road restored the adjoining dancehall and they've keep much of the rest of the Backbone just as it was under longtime previous owners. The jukebox is filled with classic country songs. The Backbone even made the pages of *Vogue* magazine, praised for its authenticity as "The Best Old-Time Honky Tonk in Texas." Maybe all those ghosts know something. It's a pretty good place to haunt.

SWINE DIVE

The former Aquarena Springs has a new eco-friendly mission in life, but whatever happened to Ralph the Swimming Pig?

There was a time when Ralph wallowed in fame. Now he's almost forgotten, a relic of simpler times when Aquarena Springs was one of the biggest tourist attractions in Central Texas and Ralph was a star. No one had yet dreamed up Schlitterbahn, Sea World, or Fiesta Texas. Even a pig could draw a crowd.

His days were numbered after Southwest Texas State University, now Texas State University, bought Aquarena Springs in 1994. Two years later, plans were underway to turn the mammoth springs into an education center. The end was near for the park's old attractions that included an underwater clown named Glurpo, diving mermaids, a submarine tourists could submerge in, and Ralph, who was actually a whole succession of trained piglets. Each was retired after it grew too large.

WATER WORLD

WHAT: Meadows Center for Water and the Environment

WHERE: 211 San Marcos Springs Dr., San Marcos, TX

COST: Tickets for half-hour glass-bottom boat tours are $9.75 adults, $6 ages 3-12. The boats, now restored, were originally used at Aquarena Springs. For schedule information, visit meadowscenter.txstate.edu/education/glass-bottomboats.html, or call (512) 245-7590.

PRO TIP: Photos and exhibits at the Meadows Center feature some of the highlights of Aquarena Springs' early years when Ralph was famous.

Ralph the Swimming Pig wallowed in fame at Aquarena Springs, but he went from stardom to hog heaven.

Top left: *Ralph the pig swam his way to stardom at Aquarena Springs.*

Top right: *The once booming tourist attraction is now part of Texas State University Meadows Center for Water and the Environment.*

Bottom: *Glass-bottom boats originally used at Aquarena Springs have been refurbished for nature tours of the springs.*

Ralph's last show was on a gray February day in 1996. There were only five people in the audience. In the end, Ralph was just another ham, but his star shined bright before he went to hog heaven.

Texas State University has been returning Spring Lake, the source of Aquarena Springs, into its original pristine condition. The second largest artesian springs in the Western United States is now part of the Meadows Center for Water and the Environment. The old Aquarena Springs Hotel is headquarters for the River Systems Institute. Glass-bottom boat tours and educational programs give visitors a look at the rare aquatic life that inhabits the springs.

HIDDEN TREASURE AROUND THE BEND

What surprise awaits you when you hike the most popular trail at Colorado Bend State Park?

When you first see Gorman Falls, it feels as if you've stumbled onto a lost world—something so surreal it looks like it belongs on a mountainside in Hawaii, or the lush big screen jungle of *Jurassic Park*. You can hear the sound of the cascade before you see it. It tumbles over a 70-feet-high drop into a lush green basin fringed with ferns and shade trees. Some say it's the most beautiful waterfall in Texas, hidden away on a remote stretch of the Colorado River, 10 miles above Lake Buchanan.

A hike down a steep, sometimes slippery trail, leads to the falls that is the centerpiece of Colorado Bend State Park. It is a "living waterfall," where stone deposits called travertine are continually increasing its 650-feet width. To protect the site, visitors have to keep their distance and no swimming is allowed.

The 5,300-acre park is a habitat for 155 species of birds, including rare songbirds and nesting bald eagles. The waterfall is its biggest treasure, but it

FINDING THE FALLS

WHAT: Gorman Falls

WHERE: Colorado Bend State Park, 2236 Park Hill Dr., Bend, TX; tpwd.texas.gov/state-parks/colorado-bend; (325) 628-3240.

COST: $5 adults, free for children 12 and under. Kayak rental is $10 per hour. Hours: 6 a.m. to 10 p.m. daily.

PRO TIP: It's a three-mile round trip to the falls. Be sure to bring water and have appropriate footwear. Reservations are recommended on busy spring days. Visit texasstateparks.reserveamerica.com/colorado-bend-state-park, or call (512) 389-8900. In late March and April, wildflowers decorate the route to the park from Llano, north on Texas 16, and northeast on Ranch Road 501.

Top: *Gorman Falls tumbles into a hidden oasis at Colorado Bend State Park.*

Inset: *It's a three-mile round trip to the falls.*

Photos courtesy of the Texas Parks and Wildlife Department

also offers an abundance of other ways to enjoy nature. Visitors kayak and fish the park's six miles of Colorado River frontage, hike its extensive trail system, and swim in the refreshing pools of Cypress Springs Creek. Gorman Falls isn't the only surprise that's hidden. The rugged, canyon-laced terrain has more than 400 caves honeycombed beneath the surface. Guided tours, offered periodically, take visitors to explore their depths.

Off-the-beaten-path, 10 miles above Lake Buchanan, Colorado Bend State Park preserves one of the state's most spectacular waterfalls.

FLOWER POWER

How did a farmer tame Texas wildflowers?

It used to be that wildflowers grew wherever nature planted them. But it wasn't so easy for everyone else who wanted to raise their own. John Thomas changed the game. Experimenting on his family's farm in Eagle Lake in 1983, Thomas began to cultivate bluebonnets and scores of other wildflowers and package their seeds. Spectacular blooms of flowers grown for seed make Wildseed Farms, his headquarters now near Fredericksburg, one of the busiest visitor attractions in the Hill Country. Spreading across more than 200 acres, it's been called the biggest flower show in Texas.

Thomas was running a company that planted grass for erosion control in the early 1980s when he began to see more demand for planting wildflowers. Getting started took a lot of trial and error. "We saw so many failures in wildflower plantings," he recalls. "There were lots of old wives' tales, but nobody knew what really worked." He spent three years and more than $500,000 to develop patented field machines that plant and harvest wildflowers. Now he produces more than 90 varieties of seeds, including a Texas Wildflower Mix that holds 28 varieties. Thomas and his staff provide consultation, seeds, and growing advice to highway

GROW YOUR OWN

WHAT: Wildseed Farms

WHERE: US 290, seven miles east of Fredericksburg

COST: Free

PRO TIP: Planting time for most wildflowers is October through November. Wildseed Farms periodically offers free planting seminars; 1 (800) 848-0078. Thomas says to find a sunny spot, with low vegetation where the seed can reach the soil, and then just toss it out "and pray for rain."

Left: *Wildseed Farms grows one of the largest flower gardens in the state.*

Inset: *John Thomas helped make it easier for thousands of gardeners to grow wildflowers.*

Photos courtesy of Fredericksburg Convention and Visitors' Bureau

departments in nearly 30 states. He has also helped develop hybrid varieties to grow bluebonnets and other popular wildflowers as far away as Holland.

Wildseed Farms has grown in all sorts of different ways too. It includes a nursery, restaurant, wine tasting room, craft and seed shop, butterfly garden, and walking trails.

With fields of flowers in bloom, Wildseed Farms puts on the biggest flower show in Texas.

GRUENE HALL'S ACE IN THE HOLE

What future country music legend earned $7 for his first performance at Gruene Hall?

George Strait and Gruene Hall go back a long way. George was a calf roper with a fresh degree in agriculture from Southwest Texas State University who wanted to give country music a try. Pat Molak had just purchased a weathered wooden dance hall in the sleepy town of Gruene in 1975. He hired George to play on Sunday afternoons, just to see what he could do. The cover charge was less than a dollar, George remembered. The future king of country music and his Ace in the Hole band earned $7 for their first show.

But soon George and his band were playing weeknights, then weekends, to bigger and bigger crowds. Both he and Gruene Hall were on their way. Gruene Hall, the oldest continuously operating dance hall in Texas, shined again, to become the centerpiece of the revived town at the edge of the Guadalupe River. George went on to an amazing string of chart-topping hits, setting a record along the way for the largest crowd ever to attend an indoor concert in North America in June, 2014, when 104,793 people heard him at AT&T Stadium in Arlington.

PAINT THE TOWN GRUENE

WHAT: Gruene Hall

WHERE: 1281 Gruene Rd., New Braunfels, TX

COST: Free, except when there's a cover charge for a performance; gruenehall.com, (830) 606-1281

PRO TIP: After you explore Gruene Hall, stop for a "gristburger," half-pound of ground beef smothered in spicy queso ($9.99) at a table overlooking the Guadalupe River at the Gristmist Restaurant next door.

Top: *Gruene Hall preserves the state's oldest continuously operating dance hall.*

Bottom: *The popular dance hall gave many musicians, including George Strait, a place to play.*

Inset: *Country legend George Strait began his career in the historic dance hall.*

The photographs for his first studio album, *Strait Country*, were shot at Gruene Hall. A signed copy hangs in an honored place among the framed photographs of many other music stars who have graced the simple stage at the edge of the dance floor. George didn't forget what it meant to him. Dance halls "are so important, especially for young singer-songwriters and bands that have just gotten together to come around and learn their trade," he told a writer for the *Dallas Morning News* when he gave a surprise concert at Gruene Hall in 2016. "I fed my family this way. I'd hate to think they were to go away, that would be tragic. What I like about this place, it never changes."

The music plays on at Gruene Hall, the oldest continuous-operating dance hall in Texas. The landmark helped bring the town of Gruene back to life as a visitor attraction.

LONG, STRANGE VOYAGE TO TEXAS

How did a wayward Japanese submarine surface and travel across America in World War II?

In downtown Fredericksburg, more than 200 miles from the nearest saltwater, a tiny Japanese submarine known as HA. 19 finally came to rest. Few vessels ever had a more star-crossed journey. The tiny sub was built as a secret weapon to join the surprise attack on Pearl Harbor on December 7, 1941. Instead, HA. 19 took a different turn and began an odyssey that would take it to towns and cities across the United States.

With a two-man crew, HA. 19 was one of five midget submarines launched for the attack. Her bad luck began that morning. With a broken gyroscope, the sub became stuck on reefs outside the harbor. HA. 19 was fired on and struck by depth charges before the lone survivor of her crew, Ensign Kazuo Sakamaki, grounded her. He was captured the following day. Ensign Sakamaki became the country's first Japanese prisoner of war. HA. 19 was salvaged for a new mission. After naval experts finished investigating the 80-feet-long, torpedo-shaped sub, it was

DIVE IN

WHAT: Japanese secret mini submarine HA. 19

WHERE: National Museum of the Pacific War, 311 E Austin St., Fredericksburg, TX; pacificwarmuseum.org; (830) 997-8600. Hours: 9 a.m. to 5 p.m. daily, except Tuesdays.

COST: $18 adults, $14 age 65 and over, $8 children.

PRO TIP: You could spend a day or more touring the major exhibits of the museum, including the Nimitz Museum that honors native son Chester W. Nimitz, who went on to become commander in chief of the US Pacific Fleet in World War II. Living history re-enactments are held on select weekends from March through November.

Top left and top inset: *Sub HA.19 toured the United States before it landed in Fredericksburg at the National Museum of the Pacific War.*

Bottom left: *Two-man crews manned the midget subs that were top secret weapons of Japan during the attack on Pearl Harbor.*

Bottom inset: *The sub became stuck on reefs outside Pearl Harbor several times before it was beached and captured.*

shipped to the mainland, loaded on a flat-bed in California and launched on a nationwide tour to sell war bonds.

Thousands of curious visitors anteed up the price of a $1 savings stamp to see the sub. From a catwalk alongside, they could view the interior through 22 viewing ports cut in the hull. They could see two life-size manikins wearing Japanese uniforms sitting at the controls with "fierce samurai expressions" on their faces. President Franklin Roosevelt was among those who saw the sub on its travels to more than 2000 cities and towns in 41 states.

After the war, HA. 19 landed at the U.S. Naval Station in Key West, Florida, and in 1991 it found a permanent home at the President George H.W. Bush Gallery at the National Museum of the Pacific War in Fredericksburg. The infamous sub is one of the prized exhibits at the sprawling museum that offers the country's most comprehensive remembrance of the Pacific War.

A wrong turn at Pearl Harbor brought a
Japanese secret submarine to the Hill Country.

BETTER MILEAGE THAN A MULE

Were camels the "Teslas" of the Texas frontier?

They could haul a 600-pound load without complaining, travel up to 60 miles in a day, and they certainly used less water than mules. Beginning in 1857, the US Camel Corps housed a herd of rangy critters at Camp Verde, about 60 miles northwest of San Antonio. The Camp Verde General Store, is a well preserved landmark from the days of that colorful experiment. It now holds a gift boutique and a popular restaurant.

Imported by ship from Egypt and the Mideast, with a crew of native drivers, the camels were used in surveying and desert crossings and by most accounts, they performed extraordinarily well. In 1857, Edward Beale led one expedition more than 1,200 miles to Fort Tejon near present Los Angeles. He reported the camels could go 36 hours without water, grazed on foul greasewood shrubs that no other animals would eat, and were almost impossible to stampede.

At Camp Verde, the dromedaries were held in a 150-feet-long corral with 10-feet-high walls. They began to fall out of favor after the Civil War. Some say the camels were put out of business by the powerful mule lobby. The opening of a transcontinental railroad also had something to do with their

---

Ahead of its time, the army used environmentally friendly experimental transportation to cross the Hill Country in the 1850s. They didn't need any gas and very little water, but soldiers had to hold their noses to ride it.

Left: *Camp Verde was headquarters for a colorful experiment by the US Army that tested the use of camels in the Southwest.*

Right: *The refurbished outpost now holds a popular store and restaurant.*

HUMP DAY

WHAT: Camp Verde General Store

WHERE: 285 Camp Verde Rd. E, Center Point, TX; campverdegeneralstore.com or (830) 634-7722

COST: Free to visit the store. The Camp Verde restaurant serves breakfast and lunch, open 8 a.m. to 4 p.m. daily. Reservations are needed on weekends.

PRO TIP: The Texas Camel Corps, located in West Texas, preserves the history of the camel experiment with education programs and camel treks. A three-day expedition in Big Bend costs $1,050; texascamelcorps/about-us.

demise, and the turmoil of the Civil War didn't help. Soldiers also complained they smelled bad. That was a serious affront coming from men who dressed in wool uniforms and bathed on a monthly basis, if then.

When Union troops took over Camp Verde in 1865, they found 66 camels remaining. Some were auctioned off to traders, others went to circuses. The army sent others to Arizona where they were used to help build the transcontinental railroad. A few escaped back to the wilds and feral camel sightings were reported up to the turn of the century. The skeleton of Beale's favorite mount, a white-haired camel named Said, was sent to Washington where it is preserved at the Smithsonian Institution's National Museum of Natural History's Hall of Bones.

CLOVIS HAS LEFT THE BUILDING

Just who was Clovis Presley anyway and was it really worth $1.50 to hear him sing?

Apparently, it was worth it. By all accounts, the newcomer put the crowd on its feet and had them hollering to the rafters when he played a show at the Cherry Springs Dance Hall on October 9, 1955. The 20-year-old Elvis Presley was so unknown that an ad in the *Fredericksburg Standard Radio Post* called him "Clovis Presley." He headlined a Louisiana Hayride show that also featured Johnny Cash, Johnny Horton, and Porter Wagoner. Tickets cost $1.50.

What a night it was. It lingers like the ghost of a faded love over the rusted roof and weathered wooden frame of the Cherry Springs Dance Hall, one of the oldest and most storied dance halls in the state. Closed since the 1990s, it sits on private property

TWO-STEP THIS WAY

WHAT: Cherry Springs Dance Hall

WHERE: 17662 N US 87, about 16 miles northwest of Fredericksburg

COST: Free to view the dance hall from the highway, but it is located on private property, not open to the public

PRO TIP: Texas Dance Hall Preservation, Inc., based in Austin, hosts annual dance hall tours and provides other information about historic Central Texas dance halls on its website, texasdancehall.org.

Turn out the lights, the party is over at the legendary Cherry Springs Dance Hall, but stars shined bright there once upon a time.

Top: *The music has faded away at Cherry Springs Dance Hall, one of the oldest and most storied dance halls in the state.*

Bottom: *Elvis Presley, then an unknown, headlined a show and was mistakenly identified as Clovis Presley. Image credit to Wikimedia Commons*

and isn't open to the public, but the landmark is easily viewed by travelers on US 87 between Fredericksburg and Mason. It was a dusty stopover on the Pinta Trail used for cattle drives when Hermann Lehmann ran it in 1889. Lehmann, the red-haired son of German immigrants, was one of the most famous Indian captives in Texas and a colorful figure on the frontier. He was the adopted son of Comanche Chief Quanah Parker.

A BAKERY RISES TO THE TOP

What will a dollar and a lone bag of flour get you?

Edouard Naegelin, a native of Alsace-Lorraine, came to New Braunfels in 1868 with small change jingling in his pocket and just enough flour to set up shop. Living above the bakery, Edouard and his wife Francisca took their craft seriously, experimenting with German and Alsatian inspired recipes. Today it is the oldest continuously operating bakery in Texas.

Come into Naegelin's Bakery and be ready to scan the glass cases full of luscious pastries. The iconic sweet treats are apple and cherry strudel, made of flaky pastry, filled with an oversupply of sweet fruit and painted with white icing. The smell of fresh baked bread hangs in the air.

With its off-white stone exterior and the blue awnings shading the balcony from the Texas daytime sun, this is the same establishment that once provided New Braunfels's residents with fresh bread delivered daily by truck to loyal customers' front porches.

What to expect in an iconic German bakery? Pfeffernusse. This is a small fragrant spice cookie often covered in frosting. Lebkuchen, a German favorite, is a thick bar cookie bathed in festive pink icing. For fans of the savory, sample the kolaches filled with your choice of sausage, cheese, bratwurst, or

---

BOUNTIFUL BAKERY

WHAT: Naegelin's Bakery

WHERE: 129 S Seguin Ave., New Braunfels, TX

COST: Bread and pastries, $1 to $6. Strudel $3 to $25. Cakes $20 to $140.

PRO TIP: Bring your children and buy them a smiley face cookie. One of the most popular items in the cases, they are a bargain at 75 cents each or a package at $7.50.

Top: *Naegelin's is the oldest bakery in Texas, operating since 1868.*

Bottom: *Pastries, pies, and cookies fill the cases in the popular bakery.*

jalapeño. For the sweet tooth, there are rolls and fruit kolaches as well as croissants. You can get a bear claw, a glazed fritter like Danish in the shape of its namesake, for a dollar.

The bakery, operated by the Granzin family since 1979, opens its doors at 6:30 a.m Monday through Saturday. Sundays it opens at 8 a.m. Get there as early as you can for the best selection.

"Good bread is the most fundamentally satisfying of all foods; and good bread with fresh butter, the greatest of feasts."
—James Beard

SNAIL MAIL SURVIVES AT HYE

Where can you get a first rate sandwich with a side of postage stamps?

The Hye Market and Post Office on US 290, 10 miles west of Johnson City, today commemorates the rich history of the area. Bring a postcard and mail it. You will be following in some famous footsteps.

President Lyndon B. Johnson was a prodigious letter writer, having put pen to paper as a small child of four to compose a letter to his grandmother. Johnson took it to the Hye Post Office. He kept up that habit throughout his life, writing 90 letters of courtship to his future wife, Lady Bird Johnson. He also posted congratulations to the high school graduates in his area.

His affinity for Hye and its people paid off for the town in 1965 when the president brought the new United States Postmaster General designee Lawrence O'Brien to the post office and had him sworn in on the wooden porch. Dignitaries and network cameras filled the narrow street. This was quite unusual for these ceremonies usually take place in or near the Nation's Capitol. The connection continued because the LBJ Ranch had box #276 in Hye, and Johnson liked nothing better than collecting his mail, pausing by the toasty stove, and having a snack of saltines and cheese.

HYE THERE!

WHAT: Hye Market and Post Office

WHERE: 10261 W US 290, Hye, TX

COST: Free admission. Sandwiches range from $7 to $13.

PRO TIP: Bring a letter to mail from the Hye Post Office. It's a great place for a family photo.

Left: *President Lyndon B. Johnson swore in a Postmaster General at the post office where he mailed his first letter as a boy.*

Inset: *The post office is a popular gathering place, serving sandwiches as well as dispatching the mail.*

When the federal government in 2011 decided to streamline postal offices, the first ones targeted were the small ones such as Hye. However, the spirit of the people of the Hill Country prevailed and saved Hye. Perhaps the continuing affection of the Johnson family for this small town played a part.

Hye is a small community of about 100 residents. Hiram G. Brown was one of the many settlers drawn to the Hill Country with its plentiful land and abundance of streams and rivers essential for survival and prosperity. Hiram, or Hye as he was called, was an entrepreneur who started a general store. Hye knew that every community needed a connection to the world at large. In 1886 he added a postal facility. This put Hye on the map and businesses followed such as a gristmill, blacksmith, and a cotton gin. Brown, who became the postmaster, moved the business and post office to a new location across the street. He remained postmaster of Hye until 1917. The current wooden building with its Bavarian inspired front was added to the Texas Historical Landmark registry in 1966.

The verdict is still out on whether Lyndon Johnson's grandmother ever received that early letter mailed from Hye. LBJ did task the Postmaster General with finding it and delivering it.

A FEISTY FOWL

How did an amorous rooster help build a unique rural icon?

Texas history is peppered with larger than life tales about legendary critters as well as mascots with personal magnetism: Bevo, Reveille, the fierce horned frog, and Cockaroo. Cockaroo may not be a household name, but his story lit up YouTube as the Castell Rooster. A large specimen, he was the amorous mascot of the Castell General Store. The big bird had a strong attraction for Billy, the famous animatronic Big Mouth Bass. Turn on the animated fish and Cockaroo would woo the bass vigorously. Cockaroo has since gone on to the big hen house in the sky, but his legend remains strong, having brought many a visitor to the store. The tough old bird has been stuffed and occupies a place of honor if you would like a selfie with him.

Castell, Texas, can boast a small but friendly community with seven full-time residents. Sitting on Ranch Road 152, it's between Llano and Mason and home to the welcoming Castell General Store. Its proximity to the Llano River is a big draw for tourists, but it also has another reason to take a flyer off the beaten path. The store sells one of the best cheeseburgers in the Hill Country, served on a sourdough bun with all the fixings. You can also dig into a grilled chicken sandwich named after the store mascot. Street tacos are on the menu, too. As well there is homemade pizza. One of its owners, local realtor and native son Randy Leifeste renovated an old gas station built in 1927 to house this store in 2008. If you need bait and tackle, come here. Rentals for

Small towns provide a bird's-eye view of the culture and history that keep these communities alive.

Top: *Castell General Store is a popular stop for travelers who want a burger and some music.*

Inset: *The store is a landmark beside the Llano River.*

kayaks and tubes are here as well. On a hot day, quench your thirst with a soda pop or one of many beers served in the rustic establishment and talk with a local resident. Cooler days encourage folks to enjoy a burger and brew at outdoors seating. You can also eat inside in the renovated feed storage room in back. The owners used wood from a dairy barn in Menard to line the walls as well as bringing in an eclectic assortment of tables and a juke box.

The owners have scheduled a recurring series of events at the store. Twice a month come for the live music. Every third week of the month, the Castell Family Church takes over the premises for informal services. Besides birthday parties and car shows, there is a chili cook off, a gumbo festival, a barbecue competition, and a beer and wine festival. However, the most unusual event is the aptly titled Testicle Festival. Pounds of calf fries and tiny turkey bits are on the menu for those folks who are not faint of heart.

COUNTRY CHARM

WHAT: Castell General Store

WHERE: 19522 W Ranch Rd. 152, Castell, TX

WHEN: Wednesday through Sunday, store opens at 9 a.m., grill opens at 11 a.m. Both close around 7 p.m.

COST: Under $10 for sandwiches

PRO TIP: Be sure to visit the nearby Llano River and view the beautiful scenery indigenous to the Hill Country.

25

ROCK OF AGES

Can you hear the ghosts calling from the summit?

Enchanted Rock is definitely in the running for favorite otherworldly phenomena. You may well hear the magnetic music of a rock expanding and contracting as it breathes a sigh of relief at the end of a hot Texas day. The sounds are the source of many legends. Do you see flickering lights at night? Could it be an ancient rekindled campfire? It's actually moonlight sparkling in the water collected in the many small pools at the summit.

However, the rock does have quite an astounding history as the scene of a standoff between Texas Ranger Captain Jack Hays and a band of Comanches in hot pursuit. Separated from his company, Hays used the rocks to hide. He was able to fend off his pursuers and in doing so, he became part of the lore of the Rangers and the rock. Look for a marker near the summit.

Rising 425 feet above its park area, it is at 1,825 feet above sea level. It's a family-friendly climb with many children using the rock pathways. The state has taken measures to preserve this pink granite mountain by limiting the number of people who can enter this natural area. You may have to wait until fellow hikers leave before you can make your ascent. Eleven miles of hiking trails are available, including the Loop and the Summit Trails. There are plenty of safe pathways to ensure your successful climb. Upon achieving the summit, look for the many small ponds covering the surface. Some of them are populated with

---

Beware: According to native legends of the region, only those with good intentions should attempt the climb.

Top: *Enchanted Rock State Natural Area preserves a mountain of solid granite.*

Inset: *The Summit Trail takes hikers 425 feet above the park.*

tiny shrimp. Home to prehistoric people 12,000 years ago, early cooks used the granite surface to pound their food. They left indentions in the hard rock that is still visible today. It is reminiscent of the moon's surface.

This imposing granite dome is 17 miles north of Fredericksburg and 24 miles south of Llano. It was declared a National Natural Landmark in 1970.

MOANS AND GROANS

WHAT: Enchanted Rock

WHERE: Enchanted Rock Natural Area, 16710 Ranch Rd. 965, Fredericksburg, TX

WHEN: Hours at the rock are 8 a.m. to 10 p.m. Trails except loop trail close 30 minutes after sunset.

COST: $8 per person 13 and up. 12 and under free.

PRO TIP: Come early to beat the crowd and allow yourself time to enjoy the small ponds and evidence of ancient dwellers at the summit. Reservations are recommended. Reserve online at texasstateparks.reserveamerica.com

CRUISING THE CANYON

Did you know that the bald eagle is a true snowbird?

If you visit the Hill Country, you'll be enchanted by the beautiful scenery and the abundance of fresh water. However, there is another big draw. Over two dozen bald eagles winter around Lake Buchanan. Once endangered, they are now fortunately off that list.

Flying at great altitudes, these birds have excellent vision and can spy a good dinner swimming in the lake. Swooping down with talons and beak on high alert, they expertly grab their prey and take off, giving folks on the river a chance to see their strength and agility in action.

These migrating snowbirds nest near Burnet, leaving in March. A great way to see these majestic creatures in flight is to take a Vanishing Texas River Cruise on Lake Buchanan. Over the years the guides and the captain have gotten to know these birds and their habits very well. Cruising the Colorado River, passengers have been treated to as many as 16 bald eagles flying overhead at one time. Of course, these magnificent birds were giving a crash course in fishing. Cruise owner Captain Shawn Devaney has 40 years experience on the river. His cruises give passengers an up close look at avian life on the water. Both of the ultimate three-hour and four-hour eagle and birding tours take passengers into the

HILL COUNTRY HEAVENLY CREATURES

WHAT: Vanishing Texas River Cruise

WHERE: 443 Waterway Ln., Burnet, TX. Boats depart from Lake Buchanan.

WHEN: Two-hour scenic tours are at 11 a.m. Wednesday, Saturday, and Sunday in August, September, and November. Longer tours are in December through February on Sunday at 9 a.m.

COST: $30 for the scenic Wilderness Cruise; $40 to $50 for the ultimate trips. (Inquire about early bird and senior discounts.)

PRO TIP: The best time for eagle watching on the cruise is in December.

Left: *Cruises take passengers to look for bald eagles and other birds.*

Right: *The Vanishing Texas River Cruise travels up the enchanting Colorado River.*

Inset: *Eagles winter along the river.*

Photos courtesy of Vanishing Texas River Cruise by Michelle Devaney

canyon to see some of the more than 600 feathered species calling the river home. Bald eagles prefer the quieter canyon areas and can often be found roosting on the rock ledges that frame the river. Folks will get a view of beautiful waterfalls as well.

Taking an excursion on the comfortable *Texas Eagle* enclosed passenger boat for a few hours gives people a chance to learn more about these beautiful creatures. Devaney recalls one encounter with an eaglet, a young eagle. Not quite as proficient as his parents in bringing home dinner, the fledgling ran into a playful coot, a small duck like bird. "That coot kept diving underwater every time the eaglet tried to get him. This went on for quite sometime with the coot winning," Devaney says.

When do you stand the best chance of truly enjoying bald eagles at the lake? Devaney says that migration patterns for species are ever changing, but that eagles usually come back to Texas skies in September.

Captain Shawn Devaney guides eagle watching tours up the canyons of the Colorado River.

ANCIENT OIL

What fruit tree yields what Homer called "liquid gold," a product once used as currency?

There is a mystique associated with olives. The trees are symbolic of friendship and peace. They are said to ensure good health as well as beauty. Olives were even buried in Pharoah's tombs.

Nestled in the Hill Country about 30 minutes outside Austin, the Texas Hill Country Olive Co. does not just sell olive oil and homemade balsamic vinegars. John Gambini and his family who bought the property in 2008 in Dripping Springs are passionate about immersing visitors in their rich Italian heritage, strongly influenced by olive oil. Their shop, restaurant, and mill are housed in a Tuscan-inspired building. In one afternoon you can learn what goes into creating first class extra virgin olive oil. However, they are now involved in a new endeavor, bringing back their orchard hit by an extreme Texas ice storm in 2021. The trees, hit hard by the freeze, are being pruned to bring them back to life by the Gambinis.

Dating back 6,000 years, olives were first grown in the Middle East, later spreading to the fertile Mediterranean region. The olive yields a beneficial oil that is prized in cooking, useful in skin care, as well as a healthy source of antioxidants. What more could one tree do? In addition, they are extremely hearty specimens, living thousands of years, providing dependable yields, and successfully surviving bad weather. They have the regenerative power of the mythical Phoenix.

TUSCANY IN TEXAS

WHAT: Texas Hill Country Olive Co.

WHERE: 2530 W Fitzhugh Rd., Dripping Springs, TX

WHEN: Monday through Sunday, 10 a.m. to 5 p.m.

COST: Tours are $8 per adult

PRO TIP: Visit the Bistro, open 10 a.m. to 3:30 p.m. Italian inspired selections are served such as pizza and antipasto.

Left: *The business includes a shop, restaurant, and mill in a Tuscan-inspired building.*

Center: *The Texas Hill Country Olive Co. processes its own oils and vinegars.*

Right: *After the freeze of 2021, the company replanted its olive orchard.*

The Gambinis have nurtured 15 acres of olive fruit trees, among them the mission and arbequina varieties. In a certified organic olive orchard, the owners have been producing extra virgin olive oil on their property in their frantoio, their authentic olive press. Guided tours are available Wednesday through Sunday at 11 a.m. through the orchard, giving the visitor a look at how trees are cultivated and how oil is produced. Expect to spend 45 minutes on the tour. If you want to know how oil is produced, take the mill tour which reveals the secrets of pressing olives to make prized extra virgin olive oil, the highest grade. This is a crash course in what it takes to produce great oil as well as preserve it. Those tours are Friday through Sunday, beginning at 11 a.m.

No wonder Thomas Jefferson extolled their virtues, "The olive tree is surely the richest gift of heaven. I can scarcely expect bread." If Jefferson came to Texas Hill Country Olive Co., he would certainly order up fresh baked bread served with an olive oil flight for tasting.

BURGERS FIT FOR A KING

Where can you always have it your way?

Elvis sightings across America are the stuff of legends. However, the King's time as an enlisted man in training in Fort Hood made it possible for the people of Central Texas to get to know him. It's no secret that Elvis Presley was a lifelong fan of comfort food. There just isn't anything more satisfying than a juicy burger and a creamy milkshake. If you wanted that meal in the early 50s and a possible encounter with the pop star, you would head for the Dairy Cue, a drive-in burger restaurant in Lampasas. More than a dozen times the carhops brought Elvis's favorite hand mixed strawberry shake to his Cadillac.

IraDell Storm and her husband J.B. opened their first drive-in on September 23, 1950, in the small town of Lampasas. Being restauranteurs runs in the family. William Washington Storm saw a need in Wood County in 1873 and filled it when he opened a stagecoach stop and post office. He enlisted his wife to helm the kitchen as she probably fed coach riders with fresh catfish and chicken fried steak, the same food she fed her own family.

The owners' son Robbis took over the Cue in 1971 while keeping up the Storm tradition of honest food. He changed the name of the 20 year-old drive-in to Storm's. The name and its iconic Storm cloud sign would become Hill Country legend. You

HALL OF FAME BURGERS

WHAT: Storm's Drive-In

WHERE: 201 N Key Ave., Lampasas, TX

WHEN: 6:30 a.m. to 10 p.m. Monday through Thursday. Closing is at 11 p.m. Friday and Saturday.

COST: Burgers cost between $4 and $9.

PRO TIP: Sit outside at picnic tables under the awning to enjoy your meal.

Left: *Storm's Drive-In has been serving burgers since the 1950s.*

Right: *Elvis Presley sometimes stopped in when he was a soldier at Fort Hood.*

knew that inside that low slung building, cooks slapped juicy beef on the hissing grill and fried never-ending baskets of sliced potatoes.

His parents had originally grown their own beef for the burgers, but as demand grew, they bought local beef. However, Storm's still grinds its own beef as it has since the beginning to ensure freshness and quality control. Although burgers have always been the calling card, the menu expanded. Robbis said that it was important to ask the customers what they wanted to eat and to provide it. Breakfast plates, Catfish and shrimp, chili dogs, chicken breast, and steak fill out the savory items. If you're looking for a culinary treat, order the Cordon Bleu Burger, a double patty stuffed with ham and cheese. The price is now higher but the most popular menu item is still the generous and meaty Storm's special. You'll get a triple decker half-pound hamburger with or without cheese along with a hearty side of the famous hand-cut French fries for under $10. It comes with your choice of fixings, made the way you like it. Finish off your meal with a sweet shake, malt, or soft serve cone. It's just like those days when Elvis came to town.

Clinton Connolly, Mike Green, and Mike Kolodzie bought the restaurant in 2013. Other locations are in Burnet and Hamilton. Storm's is in good hands for these three started out as teen carhops at the drive-in.

While many burger restaurants are a part of giant chains, Storm's carries the banner proudly and successfully for locally owned restaurants.

SURELY YOU'RE JOUSTING

What do the Hill Country, Disney World, and Bavaria have in common? A magical castle.

Taking a drive through the Hill Country, you'll enjoy the winding roads and varied topography of the region. Bonuses are the bountiful wildlife, clear streams, and abundant fish. However, a gem exists off Park Road 4 South near Marble Falls. Rising above the dense trees are the spires of a regal castle. In a state famous for historic missions such as the Alamo and huge multi-generation cattle ranches, such a bit of fairytale magic is quite an unexpected sight. How could such a place come to be in the middle of this rustic area?

Although this royal structure appears centuries old, Castle Falkenstein was actually built in 1996 by Terry Young, a developer, and his wife Kim. Their inspiration was a trip to Germany where they became enamored with Castle Neuschwanstein, a tribute

KEYS TO THE CASTLE

WHAT: Falkenstein Castle

WHERE: 7400 Park Rd. 4 S, Burnet, TX

COST: Lodging is $1,950 per night with 12 person maximum; two night minimum. With fees the stay will cost approximately $5,000. The wedding package is $4,000.

PRO TIP: For the best view, keep a sharp eye for the castle on Park Road #4. A distant view is possible for hikers in Inks Lake State Park atop the Pecan Flats Trail. Bring your binoculars.

If you are lucky enough to visit, enjoy the 360 degree view of the Hill Country from the top of the castle.

Left: *A gothic chapel with a hand-carved altar hosts weddings.*

Right: *The landmark rises in the hills near Inks Lake.*

Inset: *Castle Falkenstein was inspired by a Bavarian castle.*

Photos courtesy of Wikimedia Commons, Carol Highsmith

to composer Richard Wagner begun by King Ludwig II in 1869. Much like newspaper titan William Randolph Hearst who chose an isolated hill on the California coastline to build his castle, Ludwig used his own money to begin his magnificent retreat. Both these men discovered the folly of such an undertaking, seriously depleting their own fortunes. The Youngs took on a smaller architectural challenge but still stayed true to the elements required for a castle experience. Built out of Texas limestone, Falkenstein sits on 133 wooded acres with an unimpeded view of 30 miles of majestic Hill Country terrain. In the spring the majesty of it is framed by vibrant bluebonnets on the park road. Those fortunate enough to visit will find stone walls bordering the property, a bubbling stream, lily ponds, a well-stocked 40,000-gallon koi pond with waterfall, and butterfly gardens. One of the most memorable elements of Falkenstein is the gothic chapel with its 35-foot ceilings, hand-carved altar, and majestic arched doors.

The home boasts 14,000 square feet, six bedrooms, and four and a half bathrooms. Offered for rental to wedding parties for a day, including rehearsal time, wedding coordinator, photographers, and ceremony, couples will certainly experience being royal, if only for a day. Folks who can't make it to the Bavarian counterpart can rent Falkenstein on Airbnb for a two night minimum, enjoying the charm of the original along with the modern amenities of the Texas version.

THE TOWN
THE MAP FORGOT

How did Oatmeal get its name?

The little community founded by German settlers in 1840 came by its name as an Americanization of the name of an early area family, the Habermills. The German word for oats is Hafer. This Hill Country community expresses the can-do Texas spirit. When faced with adverse circumstances, these folks showed that sometimes it is wise to band together and put your best food forward by creatively publicizing your name.

Oatmeal is famous for its colorful water tower honoring a beloved if not exciting breakfast staple, the three minute food. Tourists seek out the colorful structure as an off-the-beaten-path photo backdrop. The 20-feet tall homage to oats came about due to a sad discovery on a newly minted Texas map back in 1978. The town had been removed because it had no intersection with major highways.

When faced with this kind of invisibility, the citizens looked for a hook to hang the town's future on. Ken Odiorne, a former mayor of neighboring town Bertram, sought out an interesting commercial possibility. Other towns had their chili cook-offs and great music venues. Oatmeal had a great sense of humor and Oats! Starting a letter writing campaign, he plead their case to all the purveyors of these rolled oats. Only National Oats answered and a water tower and, more importantly, an annual festival were born.

Luckenbach and Terlingua, Texas, had their world famous chili cook-offs. Austin has its music. However, Oatmeal had a catchy name and a love of what many Americans associate with their ancestors. In conjunction with sister town Bertram, Oatmeal invented the Oatmeal Festival held each year on Labor Day weekend. Come to the weekend party on Friday night to

OATMEAL CEMETERY

Top: *Locals saved the town of Oatmeal from being left off the map.*

Inset: *Oatmeal is famous for its colorful water tower and a festival honoring its namesake in nearby Bertram.*

FEEL YOUR OATS!

WHAT: Oatmeal Water Tower

WHERE: FM 243, 5.5 miles south of Bertram at intersection of CR 326.

COST: Free

PRO TIP: Come to the Oatmeal Festival before Labor Day, held rain or shine. The Fun Run costs from $15 to $25 depending on your age group.

experience great barbecue at the Oatmeal Community Center. Check out the historical features and interesting past of the town. Visit the old rock church and find out about the first cheese press and peach orchard in the county. The next day events include a trail ride from Oatmeal to Bertram, a pet parade, and a Grand Parade down Bertram's Main Street. It's a weekend full of luscious food, so consider the Run for Your Oats 3.3 mile race Saturday morning. It will give you a hearty appetite. If you want to sample the cooking of competitive barbecue masters, you can do that, too, at the Bertram Pavilion. Make sure you attend the Bake Off in which town experts vie for top prize in the pie and cake contests. Listen to live music at the renovated Bertram Globe Theater, a great place to escape the heat. All of this has funded college scholarships for local students as well as made community centers in Oatmeal and Bertram possible.

The effort to keep Oatmeal on the map has cemented the friendship between sister communities as well as give an old favorite breakfast food a little panache.

HISTORIC HARDWARE

Where can you get a history lesson and a new hammer?

Enter the heavy wooden doors of Henne Hardware in downtown New Braunfels and you'll swear you've stepped into the past. Original hardwood floors show the patina from many customers from different eras walking the store's aisles. Look up and you'll see an antique pressed tin ceiling, an architectural feature from the original owner, Louis Henne who was a tinsmith.

German immigrant Louis Henne was only 17 when he opened his hardware store in 1857. It is the longest continuously operating hardware store in Texas.

A two-story Victorian building constructed with two-foot-thick brick walls, this establishment has an unusual feature, a basement with its own well.

In the early days of Henne Hardware, settlers in the area could purchase a wagon to haul their goods and transport their families, buy wood-burning stoves to heat their hearth and cook their food, and find hardware to complete any necessary repairs. For any young couple contemplating

A ROOM FULL OF HILL COUNTRY HISTORY

WHAT: Henne Hardware

WHERE: 246 W San Antonio St., New Braunfels, TX

WHEN: 8 a.m. to 6 p.m. six days a week. Closed Fridays.

PRO TIP: After you visit Henne's, stop by Naegelin's Bakery for a tasty pastry.

Ask Owner Paul Martinka about the history of Henne's Hardware and New Braunfels. He is dedicated to its preservation as well as meeting the mercantile needs of the community.

Left: *The stock at Henne Hardware looks almost like a museum.*

Center: *The store stocks everything from ice cream freezers to well pumps.*

Right: *It's the oldest hardware store in the state, opened in 1857.*

marriage, Henne's was the place to shop. Known for housewares, this mercantile could outfit any home with cookware and household items.

The charm of Henne's lies in its allegiance to its past. The wooden shelves designed for displaying hardware items reach to the ceiling. Rolling wooden ladders slide along steel rails, putting everything in reach. Cash registers were not a part of early Hill Country business. The ingenuity of the Henne family brought about an overhead trolley system that shot sales tickets to the front of the store, facilitating purchases. Customers had to be alert when the trolley ran. It might just graze them on the way to its destination. You can still see what is left of the trolley lines, overlapping at the rear of the store. The custom made cabinets for small items still revolve to display their contents. Beautiful display cases house remnants from the past.

Today Henne's still serves the people of New Braunfels. The wagons of yesterday have given way to cars, trucks, and SUVS, but the store now owned by Paul Martinka keeps the spirit of friendly service alive. For those who want to enjoy fishing in the nearby Guadalupe River, get your lures, hooks, rods, and reels here. If you've got your grandchild in tow, there are plenty of toys to tempt them. If you just bought some Hill Country peaches, Henne's has an ice cream freezer to churn a few quarts for your next cookout. Hammers, nails, and shovels are all here as well.

BOOTS ON PARADE

Where can you find a Boot Hill that isn't a hill and doesn't provide a resting place for desperadoes?

A stretch of Texas Hwy 39 near Hunt, Texas, greets travelers with quite an unusual scene. Fence posts for more than two miles are topped with a continuous array of cowboy boots. These decorated posts are on both sides of this out of the way, two-lane road. Baked in the hot Texas summer sun and lashed by Hill Country rains, this footwear has seen better days.

What is behind this particular custom? Ranchers have been known to decorate their fences with any number of items. Coyote carcasses were hung to warn their hungry brethren away because those predators are the bane of a cattle rancher's existence. Snake skins were draped over wire because hanging them belly side up is said to bring rain. But boots are another matter. Boots on a post were possibly meant to alert folks that the rancher was working in that field. Another theory is that the direction the boot pointed indicated whether the rancher was at home. Another thought was that the inverted boot was in memory of a lost rancher or ranch hand.

POST TOPPERS

WHAT: Boot Hill

WHERE: Texas Hwy. 39, West of Hunt, TX

COST: Free

PRO TIP: Pull over and take a selfie. And bring an old boot.

Boot fences do not exist solely in Texas. You can find one outside the small community of Placerville, CA, as well as in Glenwood, MN.

Top: *Boots top the fence posts on a two-mile-long stretch of Texas 39 near Hunt.*

Inset: *When the footwear no longer serves its purpose, boots take their place on the road.*

What is the truth behind the Hunt Boot Hill? This Boot Hill, which is not in reality a hill, was started by a local family in the 1970s when the rancher's daughters outgrew their cowboy boots. They hung them on the fence posts. Their neighbor, finding it humorous, added to the art fence by hanging his two children's outgrown boots on his fence posts. One thing led to another and the idea caught on. Ranch hands also contributed with their worn-out boots. Neighbors topped their posts. Caught up in the desire to participate, some travelers who found Boot Hill have donated their own footwear. If you look carefully, you might find that some who donated tweaked the tradition a bit. An old laced-up work boot might be in the midst of cowboy territory. An array of colors such as pink, green, red, and turquoise punctuate the line of brown and black.

The rows of weathered leather soles speaks to the cowboy spirit in the Hill Country. It's an homage to the boot.

GRAPE EXPECTATIONS

Why do winemakers want to enlist our bare feet during harvest season?

When it's grape harvest time in the Hill Country, shed your cowboy boots and head for a vineyard. For a modest price you can recreate *I Love Lucy*'s athletic scene in a wine barrel. It's not for people skittish about getting a bath in purple juice. However, it's a great activity for those folks blessed with big feet. You will be welcomed and put to work crushing grapes.

Grape stomping is a part of the lore of winemaking. How long have winemakers been doing the stomp? The practice goes back thousands of years with earthenware jugs discovered with wine residue inside. Jugs decorated with drawings of men stomping grapes were unearthed in Tbilisi in the European country of Georgia in 2017.

Whether you call it stomping, treading, or as the French prefer, 'pigeage,' feet are involved. You've got to crush some skins to start the process. That is stomping in a nutshell. If

PURPLE TOOTSIES

WHAT: Grape stomping

WHERE: Texas Wine Country, 290 Wine Trail

COST: $15, including a T-shirt, to $65 for a T-shirt, dinner buffet, and wine

PRO TIP: Now is not the time to be prim and proper. Crush those grapes and let the juice flow. Flip flops would be an advisable "after stomp" footwear choice.

Is this toe-tickling fun sanitary? Well, grapes don't grow in a laboratory. The tangy fruit spends its days getting up close and personal with Mother Nature, including visiting birds.

Top: *Harvest time is a cause for celebration in the vineyards of the Hill Country.*

Inset: *Texas Hills Vineyard is one of several wineries that lets visitors help with the harvest.*

Bottom: *Crushing grapes takes some fancy footwork.*

you're a vintner, you study the best methods to macerate the grape's skin after the harvest. That is when the hard work begins and the path to the creation of a wine gets underway. So many wineries use machines to accomplish this and move to the fermentation process; however, there are a number of experts who extol the virtues of getting physical with the grapes. Their goal? Let the juice spend more time with the grape's skin. The theory is that with stomping you can control how many grapes or clusters you break at one time. So your feet are certainly welcome. It's all in the flavor development.

These wineries have grape stomps and wine harvests for entertainment purposes:

Texas Heritage Vineyard and Messina Hof in Fredericksburg

Hye Meadow Winery in Hye

290 Wine Castle and Texas Hills Vineyard in Johnson City

Pedernales Cellars in Stonewall

WORLD CLASS SPUR

Aren't you going to need a bigger boot?

How do you get your community recognized? Just fall back on the old brag, "Everything's bigger in Texas." That is precisely what Abe and Leah Caruthers, owners of Texas Real Estate Sales in Lampasas did. Putting their town on the map was their goal and gaining entry into the *Guinness Book of World Records* was the way to do it. Your subject must be iconic and it must be Texas sized.

Artist Wayland Dobbs of Cherokee was commissioned to bring this idea to fruition. Dobbs says he has a passion for figuring out how to make things. This would be a challenge. The subject? A gargantuan spur complete with a spinning star for a rowel. Dobbs, an artisan who is a blacksmith and metal fabricator, chose steel, copper, and iron for his materials. This combination accounts for the rust color of the sculpture. The finished product stands at 35 feet tall and is 20 feet wide. Coming in at a hefty 10,000 pounds, it rests on a concrete slab that weighs 40,000 pounds. The shank holding the revolving rowel is in the shape of legs in cowboy boots. Quite fitting!

IT'S NUMBER ONE!

WHAT: The Big Spur

WHERE: Parking lot of Texas Real Estate Sales, 1902 US 281 S, Lampasas, TX

COST: Free

PRO TIP: Take a photo under the spur's arch. It lights up for football games and special events.

The spur celebrates the state's heritage, weathering beautifully in the Texas sunshine.

Top: *The world's largest spur pays tribute to the ranching heritage of Lampasas.*

Inset: *The star tops the 35-foot sculpture by Wayland Dobbs.*

The Big Spur arrived in 2016 with a police escort, traveling from Cherokee to Lampasas. Carefully unloaded in its new home, it was lifted by a giant crane onto its platform before being bolted in place. The last piece in the puzzle was worldwide recognition. It came on February 3, 2017, when the *Guinness Book of World Records* verified that this was indeed the world's largest spur. If you build it, they will come. It's a very popular roadside attraction and well worth a visit.

A SLEEPING GIANT

What dam helped tame the Colorado River?

The Hill Country lays claim to the dam that almost wasn't. A victim of the Great Depression, this structure's future hung in the balance when funds dried up in 1932. Thanks to the creation of the Lower Colorado River Authority in 1934, work began again with the help of a benefactor. Fortunately, Congressman James Paul Buchanan stepped up and locked down federal financing for the project. Finished in 1937, it was dedicated as Buchanan Dam in honor of the congressman. The town and post office were also renamed. It became the first of six dams constructed to marshal the power of the Colorado River and crest the chain of beautiful fresh water Highland Lakes.

Heading for Highland Lakes, you'll want to see the Buchanan Dam. Two miles long and 145 feet high, it is a fine example of a multi arch dam. It was constructed to hold back lake waters, control floods, and generate hydroelectric power.

It's a powerful structure. Upon opening its floodgates, the discharge capacity is 348,000 cubic feet per second. That is quite a loud splash. As for generating electricity, its capacity is 54.9 megawatts. That will put a smile on Reddy Kilowatt's face.

To learn about this famous structure, go to the Buchanan Dam Visitor Center and Museum on SH 29 west of Inks Lake Bridge. The visitor center has an observation deck available to give you a great view of the dam and the lake. Inside the building a collection of artifacts explains the history of the dam with documents and photos.

The dam holds a reservoir Lake Buchanan that covers 20 square miles.

COLORADO RIVER
BUCHANAN DAM
WORLDS LONGEST
ARCHED 1937

A POWERFUL PLACE

WHAT: Buchanan Dam Visitor Center and Museum

WHERE: 19611 E Texas 29, Buchanan Dam, TX

WHEN: 9:30 a.m. to 4:30 p.m. Tuesday–Saturday

COST: Free

PRO TIP: The best time to look for the eagles is morning. They are busy looking for food in the afternoon.

Top: *Buchanan Dam helped bring electricity to the Hill Country when it was finished in 1937.*

Inset: *The dam was an engineering marvel when it was finished.*

Bottom: *The Lower Colorado River Authority was organized to generate power from the dam.*

While you're discovering the role played by the dam in the creation of the Highland Lakes, take a minute on the observation deck during the months from September to March to look for some iconic avian neighbors. According to Steve Buchanan of the visitor center, a bald eagle couple has made their home below Buchanan dam on the north side of the river. For the past four years they have become the neighborhood celebrities. Because these birds become attached to their homes, they have returned and added to their nests. Last year they expanded their family with two eaglets. With binoculars you may be able to see their nest which is on private land. With a lifespan approaching 25 years, these two have time left to build and rebuild, providing fans with more opportunities to watch their family grow.

DON'T GET SIDETRACKED; TAKE THE HILL COUNTRY FLYER

Is it time to let someone else do the driving?

Sign up for the Hill Country Flyer and pick your experience. Once led by steam engines, these lines now have diesel locomotives made by the giants of the 30s, 40s, 50s, and 60s.

Trains, the Iron Work Horses, have made their mark on our country. Everyone has a favorite story involving a train whether it be a ride to visit a relative or just hearing the nightly sounds of a passing flyer trailing off in the distance. We have our favorite train sayings: backtrack, sidetrack, just the ticket, and one track mind.

Trains hold a special place in people's hearts. Children are fascinated by the power of the engine and the sounds the wheels make. Adults find these work horses nostalgic. Many older passengers have family memories of forebearers who rode the rails as engineers, conductors, and porters. In their golden days trains were the most important method of transportation in America. Some of that glitter still shines when the mighty engines of the Hill Country Flyer start to roar.

You might choose the Bertram Flyer, getting your choice of seating in a vintage car from the golden age of railroads, authentically restored. This is an easy way to see some beautiful scenery while relaxing in a classic car. All aboard at 9 a.m. at the Cedar Park Depot, you'll begin your 44-mile round trip. You'll

---

Be on time! No kidding! These trains run rain or shine and wait for no one. No refunds will be given.

Left: *The train travels to Burnet, which bills itself as the Bluebonnet Capital of Texas.*

Center: *The popular Hill Country Flyer travels a route once used to bring granite to build the state capitol.*

Right: *Diesel locomotives haul vintage passenger cars on many themed excursions.*

ALL ABOARD

WHAT: Bertram Flyer and Hill Country Flyer

WHERE: Cedar Park Depot, 401 E Whitestone Blvd. C-100, Cedar Park, TX; (512)402-3830

COST: Bertram Flyer: $20 to $45. Sundays in the spring, 9 a.m. to Noon; Saturdays in the summer

Hill Country Flyer: $20 to $45. Saturdays from January to May and from September to November; 9 a.m. to 3 p.m.

PRO TIP: Bring along a sweater; the air conditioning really cools these cars.

descend into Short Creek Canyon, which is known for its rugged landscape before heading for the San Gabriel River. Crossing the river, you'll find yourself on a trestle bridge spanning 300 feet. Make sure to look below on the crossing, and you'll see huge rocks scattered on the ground. At one time this route was used to transport blocks of granite to Austin to build the Capitol. A train lost a load and the result remains below the wooden bridge. You'll stop at the Bertram Depot, a small community famous for its annual Oatmeal Festival. Then you'll return to Cedar Park Depot by noon.

For a longer trip, take the Hill Country Flyer. The most popular train trip covers 66 miles and is a round trip from the Cedar Park Depot to Burnet. Beginning at 9 a.m., this route takes riders to Burnet, with its picturesque courthouse square. There is a two-hour stopover for lunch or some shopping. The return trip takes two hours and arrives at 3 p.m.

Summers in Texas are scorchers, so, yes, the train cars are air conditioned. Drinks and snacks are available in the Cedar Park, a newly renovated concession car.

THE DOG WHO LIVED FOREVER

What small town writer turned a rescue dog tale into one of the most memorable moments in fiction?

Read the Newberry Honor–winning novel *Old Yeller* and you'll swear your house is suddenly filled with dust. The author Fred Gipson is famous for making adults and children alike reach for handkerchiefs, tears streaming down their faces.

This beloved son of the Hill Country was born in 1908 in Mason County, home to generations of German immigrants. Dangers were around every corner. Wolves and rattlesnakes shared the land and had no fear of human neighbors. This setting was the background for Gipson's tale of what we would call today, a rescue dog. A nondescript yellow dog finds its way into the heart of 14-year-old Travis Coates and his family when it wanders onto their ranch in post-Civil War Texas. Gipson with a lack of sentiment says, "He was a big ugly, slick-haired dog." Unfortunately for Travis who hankered after his own horse, his dad had other plans. "What you're needing worse than a horse is a good dog." Called Old Yeller for its color and human-sounding bark, this dog saves the day as well as a few family members several times in this classic tale.

The famous ending of the novel and the Disney movie based on the book speak to the author's and Walt Disney's belief that sadness occurs in each life and must be acknowledged and

COURAGEOUS CUR

WHAT: Mason County M. Beven Eckert Memorial Library

WHERE: 410 Post Hill St., Mason, TX

COST: Free

PRO TIP: Watch the original Disney film of *Old Yeller* before coming to town.

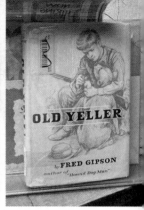

Left: *The statue at the county library honors a boy and his dog.*

Center: *Fred Gipson based many of his stories on his own experiences.*

Right: *Mason County is the setting for* Old Yeller, *a classic novel about a dog.*

respected. The death of Old Yeller is a quintessential moment in the lives of every person who has experienced Gipson's unvarnished story of love and duty. Although some in the movie industry counseled against adherence to the sad end, Disney believed in sharing the sad event of the young boy having to shoot his rabid dog. The ending shows Gipson's ability to translate the painful experiences of ranch life through the story of a boy and his dog.

Visit the Mason County Library, and you will find the artifacts and people important to the author. His desk is displayed with photos of the Gipson homestead, family members, as well as a photo of the inspiration for *Old Yeller*, which was his neighbor's dog. Sculptor Garland Weeks created a tribute in bronze to the immortal boy and his dog that greets library visitors.

Come for a visit in September on the last Saturday and participate in Old Yeller Day. The festivities include historical reenactments, arts and crafts, as well as an opportunity for children to dress up as the book's characters.

The novel and the movie underline the theme
that humans and animals share love and loyalty.

ANCHORS AWAY ON MAIN STREET

How did a Hill Country town far from the sea produce a hotel shaped like a steamboat and an admiral who led the Pacific Fleet to victory in World War II?

Anchored on Main Street in Fredericksburg, the Nimitz Hotel sticks out like a ship that's far off-course. The hotel's angular, three-story façade, topped with a flagpole, rises over other nearby buildings like the pilot house on a Mississippi sternwheeler. It was built by Charles H. Nimitz, one of the town's earliest settlers. Charles had a seafaring past—he joined the German merchant marine when he was 14. His grandson Chester, who looked up to him as a father figure after his own father died, shipped out for even bigger adventures. Taking command of the Pacific Fleet after Pearl Harbor, he became one of the country's most famous naval heroes.

The hotel, restored as part of the National Museum of the Pacific War, features exhibits that chronicle the admiral's naval career and the pivotal role he played as a commander. It also preserves the story of his colorful grandfather and the landmark hotel he built. The hotel once passed as the last scrap of civilization between the Hill Country and California. Many famous guests passed through, from future general Robert E. Lee, a frequent lodger, to the

ALL ABOARD

WHAT: Nimitz Hotel

WHERE: The hotel doesn't take lodgers, but it is open to visitors as part of the National Museum of the Pacific War, 3111 E Austin St., Fredericksburg, TX.

COST: $18 adults, $8 ages 6-17

PRO TIP: It takes at least two hours to see the highlights of the museum. Best bet is to purchase timed admission tickets online, available up to four weeks in advance; pacificwarmuseum.org; (830) 997-8600.

Top: *The Nimitz Hotel displays antiques from its early years.*

Left inset: *The hotel was built by the grandfather of Fleet Admiral Chester W. Nimitz.*

Right inset: *A statue of Nimitz stands outside the hotel that rises over Main Street in Fredericksburg.*

outlaw Johnny Ringo. It's said that the writer William Sydney Porter, better known as O Henry, hung around the bar, listening to the local German dialect, and gathering material for his short story, *The Chapparal Prince*.

The hotel grew to include a brewery, saloon, a casino-theater, a bathhouse, and a general store. Nimitz's grandfather served as a Texas Ranger and a state legislator. He loved a good practical joke. It's said that he sometimes hid silver in the luggage of a departing guest. Then he rounded up a posse to seize the baggage and open it—followed by a raucous razzing from the hotel owner. He made sure it was a hotel stay never to be forgotten.

One of Fredericksburg's oldest landmarks looks like a ship lost at sea.

MAGIC ON THE RIVER ROAD

Where can you catch a trout and follow a road that some say is the most beautiful drive in Texas?

GO WITH THE FLOW

WHAT: River Road, New Braunfels

WHERE: To reach River Road, follow Route 46 west from New Braunfels, and turn north on River Road. The road runs 12.9 miles to FM 2673. Go north on FM 2673 to Route 306 and follow Route 306 south to return to I-35.

COST: Free

PRO TIP: The Water-Oriented Recreation District of Comal County maintains an excellent web site with information on lodging, restaurants, fishing, and water flow (flow rates are determined by water releases from Canyon Lake). It hosts an annual family-oriented Fun Fish each February. Visit wordcc.com, or call (830) 907-2300. Action Angler Outdoor Center offers guided trips for experienced fly fisherman and hosts introductory lessons periodically by reservation; info@actionangler.net, or (830) 708-3474.

They call it the River Road. It doesn't go on forever, like Robert Earl Keen sings that some roads do, but you wish it would. It's that beautiful. Some say it's the best there is, in Texas at least, and maybe anywhere. Despite the fact that it doesn't have a highway number and it's well hidden, that doesn't keep football-game-size crowds from finding it on sweltering summer days, when the river is as refreshing as a tumbler of icy sweet tea. The secret is to come in the fall, when the crisp air turns the cypress trees that line the river the color of blazing lanterns and long lines of traffic are a fading memory.

For more than a dozen miles, the road hugs the Guadalupe River and brings you one beautiful view after another. Round a bend and you might glimpse a fly fisherman, standing still as a lanky great blue heron. Then he casts a silky line toward

Top: *The River Road follows the Guadalupe River.*

Left and right insets: *It is one of the most beautiful drives in the Hill Country.*

the broken water, trying to temp a hungry trout. Rainbows are stocked regularly from December through March, courtesy of the Texas Parks and Wildlife Department and Trout Unlimited. Serious fly fishers try to land them with exquisitely tied flies and some have almost as much luck as children do with a kernel of corn dipped from a can.

Down one tunnel of trees, someone draped a big American flag cars drive under. They say it's been there more than 40 years. Four bridges take you down to the water for a closer look. It's the color of liquid turquoise. There are rapids with names like Slumber Falls. Framed with high cliffs and thick woods, the Guadalupe looks like a mountain stream that tumbled off course in Colorado and found itself in the Hill Country. It's a place where nature makes the kind of magic that makes a drive well worth it.

Take a drive along the River Road in autumn and discover the secrets of a magical season.

A BLIND MAN WITH REMARKABLE VISION

How did a blind man lead a cattle drive and found a town?

Adam Rankin Johnson deserves to be remembered as a Texas legend, right up there with Travis, Bowie, and Houston. Fame is a fickle thing. Johnson—or "Stovepipe" Johnson as he was often called—was well known in his time, but you won't find any towering monuments honoring him. There's a portrait painting, posed with the green goggles he always wore, in city hall in Marble Falls, the city he founded. Airy Mount, the landmark house he built in 1884 near Burnet, was a bed and breakfast inn until recently. In 2021, it was listed for sale.

Before he lost his sight, Rankin settled near the future town of Marble Falls in 1854. He roamed all over the dangerous frontier as a surveyor and faced many encounters with hostile Indians.

REMEMBERING A HERO

WHO: Adam Rankin "Stovepipe" Johnson

WHERE: Airy Mount, Johnson's house, 1819 E Polk St., Burnet, TX (on Texas 29, about 1.3 miles east of US 281), the house is privately owned, but it can be seen from the highway.

COST: Airy Mount, the Johnson Barn and another historic home on 5.76-acres were listed at $1.9 million in 2021.

PRO TIP: You can find photographs and more information about Johnson at the Falls on the Colorado Museum in Marble Falls.

Marble Falls was once known as "the blind man's town," but its founder was a man of remarkable courage and vision.

Top: *Airy Mount was the last home Adam Johnson built.*

Inset: *Blinded by his own men near the end of the Civil War, Johnson came home to the Hill Country to found the town of Marble Falls.*

He was fascinated with what was then the "great marble falls" of the Colorado River. He believed the river had great potential as a power source. On rocks on opposite sides of the river above the town site, he scratched crosses for the site of a future dam. More than 70 years later, the massive Buchanan Dam was built there.

Johnson went off to organize a cavalry unit in his native Kentucky after the outbreak of the Civil War. His dashing exploits helped him rise to the rank of brigadier general. In one raid that earned him his nickname, Johnson captured a Union arsenal in Indiana with a small force and two fake "cannons" made with stovepipes. Near the end of the war he was accidentally blinded by a shot fired by his own men.

Blind, penniless—and undaunted—Johnson returned to Texas. He organized cattle drives and led them, and sold lots for his new town. He pioneered the granite industry and gave land for a railroad to deliver stone to Austin to build the state capitol. Johnson died in 1922 and is buried at the Texas State Cemetery in Austin. In spite of his lack of sight, he was a man of remarkable vision and, as one of his friends said, "perhaps no man has led a more cheerful and happy life."

BUSY BEES

What kind of wildflowers do honeybees love the best?

Surprise. It isn't bluebonnets. The state flower draws swarms of springtime tourists to the Hill Country, but honeybees just pass the masses of blossoms by. "They can't access the nectar," explains Clint Walker, who owns Fain's Honey Company, a nearly century-old business headquartered between Burnet and Llano. Fortunately, they're fond of other flowers that are plentiful too. "They like Indian blanket and horsemint," Clint says, "and they like yucca blossoms too." Bee brush, also known as white brush, a brush country plant that produces delicate white flowers through the spring and summer, is also a bee delicacy.

Those are some of the blossoms that bees use to produce Fain's natural raw pure honey. The popular product, little changed since the 1920s, is sold in shops and at H-E-B stores across Central Texas. At the Fain's Honey factory and headquarters store, 55-gallon barrels of honey gathered from hives and mixed in a proprietary blend are warmed, filtered, and bottled. "Basically we just filter out the larger particles and bottle it," Clint says. "We want to get that nice golden color. We're packaging raw honey."

A TASTE OF HONEY

WHO: Fain's Honey Company

WHERE: Factory store, 14817 Texas 29, Buchanan Dam, TX

COST: $13.95 for a 3-pound jar of Fain's Natural Raw Pure Honey

PRO TIP: H-E-B stores and many shops in the Hill Country stock Fain's Honey, but the factory store has the widest selection of products. A popular Hill Country gift assortment includes raw honey, peach honey butter, cinnamon honey butter, and pecan honey butter, $37.75. The store opens 9 a.m. to 6 p.m. Monday–Friday, and 9 a.m.–4 p.m. Saturday; fainshoney.com; (512) 793-2491.

Top: *The honey is sold in many stores throughout the Hill Country, but the factory offers one of the widest selections of products.*

Inset: *Fain's Honey has been harvesting one of the Hill Country's sweetest crops for almost a century.*

Clint, whose family has owned Walker Honey in Bell County for generations, bought Fain's Honey in 2021. He plans to continue the traditions Fain's Honey has followed since H.E. Fain started the business in 1926. The company still gathers its own honey from hives in Central Texas. "We spend the year following the blooms," Clint says. Pesticides and other ills have taken a toll on bee populations nationwide, but the all-important pollinators are holding their own in Central Texas. Too bad they don't have a taste for bluebonnets. "That would be perfect," says Clint. "Bluebonnet honey. People would love it."

Fain's Honey has been gathering its sweet product in the Hill Country for almost a century.

FORGOTTEN PEACEMAKER

How did a Hill Country town wind up with the name of a Comanche chief?

With a population of less than 100, Katemcy is an unincorporated town with only a few weathered buildings clinging to the rugged granite hills north of Mason. It's a name that's almost lost in time, and that's a shame, because it ought to be celebrated. When violence raged between Comanches and settlers in the Hill Country, the town's namesake was a chief who took a different trail. He was a peacemaker.

John Meusebach, the founder of Fredericksburg and leader of German settlers moving into the Hill Country in the 1840s, took a different trail too. He came in peace. Meusebach led a scouting party that met with the Comanches in 1847. Katemcy led members of the Penateka (Honey Eaters) band. They were the most powerful and feared band of Comanches at the time. With Katemcy in the lead, they carried a white flag. Eventually the Penatekas signed

WHAT'S IN A NAME

WHAT: Katemcy

WHERE: Ranch Rd. 1222, one mile east of US 87, Mason County

COST: Free

PRO TIP: The landscape around Katemcy is still rugged. It once was used by Katemcy Rocks for one of the most extreme off-road challenges in the state. Visit katemcyrocks.com.

Chief Katemcy led his people in peace and helped open up 5,000-square-miles for German settlers.

Top: *Katemcy is almost a ghost town now.*

Left inset: *In 1847, German settlers met in the remote countryside to offer a treaty to the Comanches.*

Right inset: *The town took its name from a Comanche chief who helped bring peace to the Hill Country.*

one of the most lasting treaties in the history of the west. It opened more than 5,000-square-miles to settlement—some four million acres that formed parts of 10 Texas counties.

Settlers eventually came to the rock-rimmed ravines at Devil's Springs that once was Katemcy's winter camp. When Alfred Cowan became postmaster in 1884, the town needed a name. Cowan is said to have jokingly suggested "Hammersville," because there was so much noise from new buildings going up. Postal authorities rejected that. There were already too many "villes," they said. Another name was proposed—Ketemoczy—that was the German spelling of the chief's name. Postal authorities liked the sound of it, but they changed the name to Katemcy, because it was more phonetic. By that time, the peacemaker was long gone. He continued to make peace to the very end, leading his people first to a reservation in North Texas, and when that was attacked by bushwhackers, on to a reservation in what would become Oklahoma. All that he left behind was his good name.

HEALING WATERS

Where can you splash in the oldest spring-fed swimming pool in Texas?

Framed by massive pecan trees, the historic Hancock Spring-Fed Swimming Pool in Lampasas is said to be the oldest in the state. Native Americans believed in the healing powers of the springs and made pilgrimages to soak in them. When the first Anglo settlers came, the springs became so popular by the late 1800s that Lampasas was called "the Saratoga of the South."

Investors built a grand, two-story, 200-room Park Hotel on a rise above Sulphur Creek. A new railroad line brought carloads of visitors. Mule-drawn trolley cars carried them from the downtown station to the Park Hotel and six other hotels in town. An elaborate bathhouse provided bathing facilities for male and female guests. The cut-stone ruins of the bathhouse still stand at the edge of Sulphur Creek. In the early days, baths cost 15 cents.

JUMP IN

WHAT: Hancock Spring-Fed Swimming Pool

WHERE: 1406 US 281 S, Lampasas, TX

WHEN: The pool is generally open in July and August, but schedules vary due to lifeguard availability. For hours, visit lampasas.org, or call (512) 556-6831.

COST: $3.50 adults, $2.50 seniors and children

PRO TIP: Neighboring the pool, the waters of Cypress Creek also frame Hancock Springs Golf Course, which features a signature "island" green. The downtown square preserves the town's landmark courthouse and many other historic buildings.

The mineral waters of Hancock Springs once brought visitors to Lampasas by the train load. The resort town hosted the state Democratic Convention in 1892.

Top: *Healing springs made Lampasas a resort town in the 19th century.*

Left inset: *Hostess House, once a gathering place for dances and parties, is preserved as a bathhouse.*

Right inset: *The popularity of Hancock Springs gave rise to hotels, and Lampasas hosted many gatherings, including the state Democratic Convention.*

Spring water, flowing at the rate of 70 gallons a second, fills a natural bottom pool, opened in 1911. The water flows through the pool and returns to the creek. It stays a chilly, 70 degrees year-round, and the mineral water has a sulfur smell. The waters were a balm for soldiers during World War II when the pool and Hancock Park served as a rehabilitation center for nearby Fort Hood, then called Camp Hood when it opened in 1942. Flanking the front side of the pool, the historic, limestone-clad Hostess House is a restored landmark still used as a changing house for swimmers. Its second floor is a setting for weddings and other events now, but it was once an open air dance pavilion that filled the park with the music of many well-known bands and singers almost a century ago. On a hot summer afternoon, when you hear the laughter of children splashing in the cold, clear water, the pool itself sounds like an old sweet melody of summer, a gift treasured and handed down, from long ago.

HAPPY HOUR AT THE P.O.

How can you operate a post office in a saloon?

You could start by offering the postal inspector a drink too. That's one of the family legends about the way enterprising storekeeper Hermann Fischer was able to keep operating one of the few post offices in the country with a saloon in the same building. Hermann had tradition on his side. After immigrating from Germany, he opened his general store in a scenic setting in the rugged hills of northern Comal County in 1853. He and his brother Otto were the first settlers in the area and the store was a welcome outpost on the frontier. It thrived, eventually employing 16 clerks, to become one of the state's largest mercantile establishments in its early days.

The present store was built in 1902 and enabled Hermann to move the saloon into a separate building, where it operated until Prohibition. Inside the Fischer Store, original display cases hold antiques and dry goods that were stocked more than a century ago.

Weather information was one of the services the store provided. Record keeping began in 1887. The store survived the Great Depression, but the 1950s drought tested the limits of perseverance. Wells dried up and crops withered. "Need rain to survive," descendant Eddie Fischer wrote in the weather ledger just before the drought broke in 1957.

KEEPING STORE

WHAT: Fischer Store

WHERE: 4040 FM 484, Fischer, TX

COST: Free

PRO TIP: The store sometimes opens from 10 a.m. to 4 p.m. on Saturdays, but it's best to check in advance. Visit fischerstore.com or call (830) 370-1554. Information is also available at facebook.com/fischerstoresaturdaymarket and facebook.com/fischerdancehall. The store is 12 miles southeast of Blanco on Texas 32.

Top: *The Fischer Store has been an outpost in Comal County since 1853.*

Bottom: *Fischer Hall was built to host dances and community gatherings.*

Beginning with the store, the community of Fischer expanded to include a school, a hall for community events, and a bowling club for old-style, nine-pin bowling, favored by German settlers. All still stand. Fischer Hall, built with rafters that span the width of a wide dance floor, hosts weddings, reunions, and dances. Family descendants operate the store as a museum.

Fischer Store stands as an iconic landmark on a scenic drive between San Marcos and Blanco.

TEXAS-SIZED CHRISTMAS ORNAMENT

What is that giant wooden spinning thing that lights up in the middle of Fredericksburg each holiday season?

It's called a Weihnachtspyramide, or Christmas pyramid. Standing as tall as most of the historic buildings on Main Street, the 26-feet-high structure is a magical-looking holiday centerpiece of Marktplatz park downtown. It was imported from Germany where it was put together by craftsmen and assembled in Fredericksburg in 2009.

The Christmas pyramid is a giant-sized duplication of the table-top Christmas pyramids most people are familiar with. It's similar to the candle-powered, windmill-topped ornament Cousin Eddie accidentally dismantled in *Christmas Vacation*. The lofty wooden blades on the Fredericksburg ornament rise above five levels of near-lifesize carved figures that rotate around the base. Shepherds, nutcrackers, snowmen, and other characters move to the music of the Dance of the Sugar Plum Fairy. Children are fascinated by it.

Originally, the Christmas pyramids were built to teach children Bible stories. They originated in the German Erzgebirge (Ore Mountains). It was once a mining region, but when the mines played out, workers began the business of crafting wooden toys. Christmas

WHAT GOES AROUND

WHAT: Christmas pyramid

WHERE: Marktplatz park, 100 block of Main Street, Fredericksburg, TX.

COST: Free

PRO TIP: The 55 Nights of Lights celebration starts the day after Thanksgiving. Activities include a skating rink at the Marktplatz. Some shops sell table-top Christmas pyramids, including The Grasshopper and Kuckucks Nest.

Top: *Fredericksburg Christmas pyramid, standing 26 feet high, is the centerpiece of the town's Christmas celebration. Photo courtesy of Fredericksburg Convention & Visitors Bureau*

Left inset: *Life-size carved figures rotate around the base.*

Right inset: *The Christmas pyramid was imported from Germany and assembled by craftsmen from Europe.*

pyramids grew out of their early efforts. Since it was installed in 2009, Fredericksburg's Christmas pyramid proved so popular, German craftsmen have built large-scale versions for several other cities, including Dallas, and towns in Alabama and Colorado.

Most Christmas pyramids can fit on a tabletop, but one in the Hill Country is as tall as a building.

A TRIP TO BLANCO MAKES SCENTS

Why do motorists roll down their windows and take deep breaths when they drive through Blanco?

It smells heavenly when the lavender is in bloom. So many farms dot the countryside that Blanco is known as the "Lavender Capital of Texas." The plants generally flower from May through July. The Blanco Lavender Festival (scheduled for June 10–12, 2022) celebrates the harvest with farm tours, music, and booths filled with plants and products on the courthouse square.

Hill Country Lavender, the oldest commercial farm, got its start in 1999 when *National Geographic* photographer Rob Kendrick and author Jeannie Ralston planted the first fields. They were inspired to try growing lavender in Texas after visiting some of the lavender-growing regions in France, where the soil and climate were similar to the dry weather and alkaline limestone soil of the Hill Country. It was a match made in heaven. Soon fields of lavender were crowned with violet blossoms all around Blanco. Jeannie and Rob helped start the lavender festival. Tasha Breiger, who once managed their farm, planted larger fields at Hill Country Lavender. The

PAINT THE TOWN PURPLE

WHAT: Lavender Capital of Texas

WHERE: Blanco Lavender Festival, June 10–12, 2022; blancochamber.com, (830) 833-5101

COST: Roundtrip shuttle to Hill Country Lavender is $5 per person during the festival. The farm at 8241 Farm Road 165 is open from 10 a.m. to 4 p.m. Thursday–Saturday

PRO TIP: If you're thinking of planting your own lavender, the festival is a good place to get started. Booths on the square sell plants and experts offer advice on growing them.

Top: *Hill Country Lavender grows a bumper crop of the fragrant plants.*

Left inset: *The landmark courthouse is the centerpiece of the Blanco Lavender Festival held each June.*

Right inset: *Blanco is known as the lavender capital of Texas.*

farm, which is open for tours, is one of the centerpieces of the lavender festival. In addition to selling plants, it produces dozens of lavender products, ranging from soap to lavender tea.

According to *Southern Living Magazine*, sales of lavender products and plants soared during the Covid-19 crisis because of their soothing aromas. When you pass through Blanco when the fields are at their peak, you don't even have to buy anything. Just roll down your windows and breathe.

The town of Blanco grows its own perfume.

WHOPPER OF A FISH STORY

How did a small town park land a fish so big it took a truck to deliver it?

Pickup trucks carry all sorts of loads in Texas, but one in Lampasas is saddled with a cargo so strange it's a traffic stopper. Draped over the truck bed and stretching high over the top of the cab is a whopper of a catfish. Joe Barrington's *Been Fish'en* is one of the centerpieces of Hanna Springs Sculpture Garden. The sculpture garden in Campbell Park is a small town surprise filled with whimsical artworks, delightful for families and children.

Barrington's catfish, hauled by a rusting 50s Chevy pickup, is one of the largest pieces. Not far away, colorful metal butterflies spin on mobiles in David Hickman's sculpture, *Meadow Dances*. There is a totem stacked with birds, and giant, bright flowers. A sculpted flying horse, *Pegasus* by Carolann Haggard, soars nearby.

Local artist Nancy Gray proposed the garden and it opened in 2005 under the

FISH FACTS

WHAT: *Been Fish'en*, fish sculpture, Hannah Springs Sculpture Garden

WHERE: 501 E North Ave., Lampasas, TX

COST: Free

PRO TIP: If you like a sculpture in the garden, you might be able to take it home with you. Occasionally, the garden shows art works that are for sale. For information on sales and art events, visit the arts association at lafta.org/sculpture-gardens.html; or call (512) 525-9173.

Visitors fall for the Hanna Springs Sculpture Garden hook, line, and sinker.

Top: *There are many kinds of sculptures to catch your eye at Hanna Springs in Sculpture Garden in Lampasas.*

Inset: *It's tempting but the catfish is off limits to children.*

Bottom left: *More than 20 art projects decorate the sculpture garden.*

Bottom right: Pegasus *by Carolann Haggard soars on its pedestal.*

direction of the Lampasas Association for the Arts. Three artists carved their sculptures on site. They include Carolann Haggard's *Lampasas Furniture*, made of limestone, T.J. Mabrey's *IV Florae for Flora*, and David Hickman's *Portal to the Springs*, massive carved blocks topped with a mobile fish. Funded by donations or donated by the artists themselves, more than 20 sculptures decorate the garden now. Several times during the year, the arts association hosts shows and participatory art events for families.

TREASURE FOR THE TAKING

Did Jim Bowie die at the Alamo with a map in his pocket guiding the way to a fortune in silver hidden in the Hill Country?

That's one of the more intriguing legends of the Lost Bowie Mine. Folklorist J. Frank Dobie mentioned it in *Coronado's Children*, filled with tales of lost riches that got treasure hunters salivating nearly a century ago. He wasn't the first to spark the fever. In 1756, Spanish explorer Bernardo de Miranda y Flores pulled up samples from a shaft he claimed was so bountiful everyone in the Spanish territory of what became Texas could have a mine of their own. When Stephen F. Austin was trying to attract settlers, he hawked the treasure story too. He put the location on his 1829 map, but he put it in the wrong place.

For almost three centuries the lost mine had many names and more locations than an Amazon driver could reach in a month of Sundays. Bowie and his brother Rezin made at least two expeditions to try to find it. One of them brought on one of the most harrowing Indian fights on the frontier, but Bowie and most of his party survived. They were

DIG IN

WHAT: Lost Bowie Mine

WHERE: One popular theory is that the mine is located on Honey Creek, five miles east of the Oxford Cemetery on Texas 16 between Llano and Fredericksburg. Former exploration sites are on private property.

COST: Priceless

PRO TIP: Even if you don't find treasure, Texas 16 is one of the Hill Country's most beautiful drives in spring when wildflowers decorate the roadsides. Don't miss the Willow City Loop, which circles off the highway into ranch country, but it can get crowded on weekends.

Top: *Treasure hunters have scoured the Hill Country for the Lost Bowie Mine, including one location near the Oxford Cemetery.*

Left inset: *The Oxford Cemetery rests in peace near Llano.*

Right inset: *Legend says Bowie may have died at the Alamo with a treasure map in his pocket.*

headed for the ruins of the abandoned Spanish presidio at Menard near the San Saba River, where they believed the mine was located.

Some believe they were way off course. A treasure hunter in 1902, using archives obtained from Mexico, pinpointed Miranda's original exploration at Honey Creek, about 12 miles south of Llano and more than 70 miles from Menard, where the Spanish built a presidio and mission before the priests there were massacred by the Comanches. Many paid a high price for a priceless treasure, but it's such a tempting prize, the searching has continued right up to the present.

Swashbuckling Jim Bowie carved his legend across Texas, but he never found the treasure he was looking for.

A DAY MADE FOR A SUNDAY HOUSE

Did German farmers plant the first seeds of the tiny house movement in Fredericksburg almost a century ago?

They are tiny, usually just two rooms, with a loft, and an outside staircase, to save space. Sunday Houses are prized in Fredericksburg, where about 100 of them dot the historic district around Main Street. They don't exist in Germany or many other places in the world. German farmers invented them not long after the town was settled. They were born out of necessity. When they came to town with their families on weekends to buy goods and attend church, they needed a place to stay.

When Fredericksburg was settled in 1846 by the Society for the Protection of German Immigrants in Texas, each family head was given a town lot and 10 acres of farmland. It was expected that farmers would tend their land, then come back to town each evening. That proved impractical. It was too difficult to travel back and forth. Tiny, practical Sunday Houses remedied the problem. They were usually 1 ½ stories tall, with a sleeping loft for children. There was a fireplace for heating, and a rudimentary lean-to kitchen, or no kitchen at all, and no water.

Some streets were lined with Sunday Houses, built from the 1830s up to the 1930s. Many were clustered around churches. One of the largest remaining groups is near St. Mary's Catholic Church on West San Antonio Street. A number of others are on West Main and South Milam Streets.

Some very small houses occupy a big place in the heart of Fredericksburg.

Left: *The house is part of a complex of vintage-style Sunday houses.*

Right: *The Loeffler-Weber Haus, one of the oldest houses in Fredericksburg, operates as a bed and breakfast now.*

"What killed the Sunday Houses was the automobile," local historian Glen Treibs told *Forbes Magazine* in 2021. "They were a solution to the problem of traveling long distances in harsh conditions, and cars pretty well took care of that."

But the same changes that ended their original purpose also gave them a new lease on life. Travelers, who began to flock to Fredericksburg on smooth, new roads, found them charming. The majority of the survivors have been preserved as weekend getaways and guest houses. A number of new guest houses have been built in the style of the old Sunday Houses. One of the oldest, the Weber Sunday House, is preserved for public viewing at the Pioneer Museum.

STAYING SMALL

WHAT: Sunday Houses

WHERE: Weber House, Pioneer Museum, 325 W Main St., Fredericksburg, TX

WHEN: Monday–Saturday, 10 a.m. to 5 p.m, visit pioneermuseum.net, or call (830) 990-8441

COST: $7.50 adults, $3 ages 6–17

PRO TIP: Experience what life was like for the first settlers—with many conveniences added—at the Loeffler-Weber Haus, one of the first Sunday Houses built in 1846. Rates start at $299 per night; stayfredericksburg.com, or (325) 247-0098.

A FORT FILLED WITH FUTURE GENERALS

What Hill Country frontier fort produced 20 generals for both sides in the Civil War?

George Stoneman was one of them. Don't recognize his name? Try this, "Virgil Cane is my name and I served on the Danville train. Till Stoneman's cavalry came and tore up the tracks again."

In command of Union cavalry, Stoneman led a 600-mile raid across North Carolina and Virginia toward the end of the Civil War. A hero of the war, he later became the 15th governor of California.

On a hilltop overlooking the town of Mason, you can see the restored officers' quarters that was once home to Stoneman and 19 other future generals who served at the outpost. In 1856, the fort was the headquarters for seven companies of the elite 2nd Cavalry. That fighting force was the pride of the army. Everyone wanted in. Fort Mason was its regimental headquarters numerous times. Among the future generals it produced, 12 fought for the Confederacy, eight for the Union. They included Earl Van Dorn, Fitzhugh Lee, E. Kirby Smith, George H. Thomas, John Bell Hood, William J. Hardee, and Philip St. George Cooke.

MAKING GENERALS

WHAT: Fort Mason

WHERE: 204 W Spruce St., Mason, TX

COST: Free

PRO TIP: The sturdy stone fort once included more than a dozen buildings. After it was deactivated in the 1870s, many of the rock building materials were repurposed by settlers into landmark homes that still stand. The nearby Mason County Museum and the Museum on the Square showcase the town's colorful history. Hours vary and the county museum closes in winter; masonsquaremuseum.org.

Top: *Fort Mason was home to 20 officers who later became generals.*

Inset: *Robert E. Lee was once stationed at the fort.*

But the most famous future general at Fort Mason was its last commander. In The Band's 1969 classic song, "The Night They Drove Old Dixie Down," Levon Helm sang about him too. "Virgil, quick come see, there goes Robert E. Lee." He was passing in defeat. Fort Mason was Lee's last command, before he was summoned to Washington and offered command of the Union army, which he turned down. The Civil War soon began. The men at Fort Mason were brothers in arms, but they were destined to do battle against each other. It's a sad song, Levon Helm sings. No one ever said it better.

The soldiers at Fort Mason protected the frontier, but in the end, they fought each other.

HIGH PRICE FOR COMFORT

Why does one American flag always fly at half mast in the town of Comfort?

Many of the German pioneers in the Hill Country fled strife and persecution in their homeland. They weren't ready to turn their backs on a new country they loved. They were loyal Americans.

When the Civil War erupted, German settlers in towns across Central Texas paid a high price for their loyalty. Some historians say as many as 150 were lynched or shot. In Comfort, a tall limestone obelisk is engraved with the names of 36 who died in the Nueces Massacre and its aftermath.

By 1862, passions were so enflamed that some 70 loyalists set out for Mexico. They were camped on the Nueces River on August 10 when they were attacked before dawn by around 100 Confederate irregulars called Duff's Partisan Rangers. The attackers were commanded by James Duff, a shadowy character who was a US Army deserter

LOYAL TO THE END

WHAT: Treue Der Union Monument

WHERE: High Street between 3rd and 4th in Comfort, near the high school

COST: Free

PRO TIP: It's worth a trip to see Main Street in Comfort, one of the most picturesque collections of 19th century limestone landmarks in the Hill Country.

Many German settlers in the Hill Country remained true to the Union during the Civil War. In Comfort, a monument honors some who paid with their lives.

Top inset text:
Gefallen am 10 August 1862 am Nueces
L. Bauer,   J. G. Kalenberg,
F. Behrens,   H. Markwart,
E. Beseler,   C. Schafer,
L. Borner,   L. Schierholz,
A. Bruns,   H. Steves,
H. Degener,   W. Telgmann,
H. Degener,   M. Weirich,
P. Diaz,   H. Weyershausen,
F. Vater,   A. Vater,
A. Schreiner.

Top: *A Limestone obelisk honors the loyal patriots of Comfort.*

Top inset: *More than 30 brave citizens died in the Nueces massacre and its aftermath.*

Bottom inset: *The sanctuary honors German settlers who were true to the Union in the Civil War.*

himself. Nineteen of the loyalists were killed in the battle. Prisoners were executed. Accounts are conflicting on how many were shot, but at least 17 more were killed after the battle and at a subsequent fight on the Rio Grande, where a number were drowned.

At the war's end, their remains were gathered and a monument rose in Comfort to honor their sacrifice. At its top, the German words, "Treue Der Union," record their "Loyalty to the Union." Beside it, a flag with 36 stars flies permanently at half staff, one of the few memorials in the US to accord that honor.

DISAPPEARING MOUNTAIN

Granite Mountain once was one of the tallest landmarks in Marble Falls. Where did it go?

Granite Mountain isn't as big as it used to be, but you can find pieces of it in towering buildings all over the world. The Sears Tower in Chicago, once the country's tallest building, has some. So does Grand Central Station in New York and the Coca-Cola Building in Atlanta. Huge chunks of it anchor the jetties that help hold back the sea in Galveston. The monumental Texas state capitol is also built with sunset red granite.

Rising out of the landscape in a solid dome known as a bomhardt, Granite Mountain once rose 200 feet high. A century and a half of quarrying has reduced its size, but more than enough remains to last at least another 2,000 years, geologists say. It is a geological sister of a larger, more famous granite dome, Enchanted Rock, near Fredericksburg. They were both created from magma chambers of igneous rock deposited deep below the surface more than 1 billion years ago. The Enchanted Rock batholith stretches more than 60 miles underground. The rock in Granite Mountain extends far below the surface too.

William Ransom Slaughter, one of its first owners thought it wasn't worth "a packsaddle and the mule I'm leading." He sold it to George W. Lacy for a little over $3,000 in 1882. Lacy formed a partnership with Adam Johnson. Then they brokered a deal

There's more to Granite Mountain than meets the eye. Central Texas may have the second largest deposit of granite in North America, but most of it is far below the surface.

Left: *Granite Mountain in Marble Falls supplied stone for the state capitol and many other monumental buildings.*

Right: *The mountain once rose 200 feet high. It is said that still holds enough stone to last another 2,000 years.*

to give a monumental amount of the granite away. The stone was to be used to build the state capitol. In return the state built a railroad spur to help bring the rock to Austin and furnished 300 convicts to work for 65 cents per 10-hour shift. They helped cut 50,000 tons of granite, enough to fill more than 15,700 railroad cars that were sent to Austin. Massive granite blocks that sometimes tumbled off the cars still dot the railroad line.

Cold Spring Granite Company of Cold Spring, MN, operates the quarry and half a dozen other sites in the Llano Uplift now. Each produces a different color of granite. Some of the other colors are radiant red, Indian sunset, sunset beige, Texas pearl, and Texas pink. Many Texans, and even a few guidebooks, contend the Texas capitol is built with pink granite, but its true color is sunset red.

ROCK SOLID

WHAT: Granite Mountain

WHERE: One mile west of US 281 on Ranch Road 1431

COST: Free to view from a small roadside turnoff on the highway where the history of the mountain is chiseled on a granite slab.

PRO TIP: The quarry isn't open to the public, but the Falls on the Colorado Museum at 2001 Broadway in Marble Falls displays many historic photographs of quarry work on the mountain.

QUIET PLEASE, CATTLE DRIVE PASSING THROUGH

Where can you ride the range across Texas in the quiet comfort of a library?

Most libraries ride herd on books, but when you step through the doors of the Wittliff Collections on the 7th floor of the main library at Texas State University, you half expect a herd of rangy longhorns to come charging out. The library is the stomping grounds of Woodrow Call, Gus McCrae, and a wild bunch of other rowdy Texas cowboys. Many of them tumbled out of the imaginations of the late Bill Wittliff, Larry McMurtry, and other famed Texas writers featured in the collections.

Wittliff was the screenwriter for the Emmy-award-winning series, *Lonesome Dove*. He donated his own collection of scripts and props and convinced most of the crew to do the same. They handed over enough memorabilia to make the permanent exhibit of *Lonesome Dove* look like a movie set.

Wittliff and his wife Sally began rounding up their

CHECK IT OUT

WHAT: Wittliff Collections

WHERE: 7th floor, Albert B. Akek Library, Texas State University, 601 University Dr., San Marcos, TX

COST: Free. Open daily on weekdays and afternoons on weekends.

PRO TIP: Be sure to see The History of Ranching, Buck Winn's panoramic mural on the ground floor of the library. Originally commissioned by the Pearl Brewery in San Antonio, it was one of the world's largest murals when it was completed in 1950. An 82-foot section, restored by the Wittliff Collections, is suspended from the library ceiling.

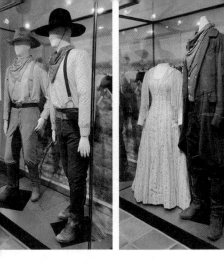

Inset: *The museum holds the world's largest collection of props from* Lonesome Dove.

Left: Lonesome Dove *characters stand tall at the Wittliff Collections at Texas State University.*

Right: *The exhibit features clothing worn by many of the film's characters.*

phenomenal collections of Texas and Southwestern photography, music, and literature in 1986. They gathered everything from hand-penned song lyrics from Willie Nelson to one of the earliest records of exploration in Texas, published in 1755 by Cabeza de Vaca. They brought in writer's collections from folklorist J. Frank Dobie, novelist Cormac McCarthy, screenwriter Sam Shepard, and many others.

Treasures of the Wittliff showcases highlights of the collections, including the shipwrecked de Vaca's *La Relation*, one of the world's rarest books.

Fans come from far-flung places to see the *Lonesome Dove* exhibit. In one video, Wittliff recalls that film financiers wanted to have Gus and Woodrow herd goats, instead of cattle. They wanted to have the cattle disappear in a stampede and have the pair say, "Well, there goes our herd." The cattle stayed, and fortunately even turned a profit, because prices went up during the filming. Episodes from the series play on in a small theater. If the action carries you away, it's a library where it's OK to let out a "whoop" every once in a while.

The spirits of legendary Texas cowboys roam the halls at this library.

RIDE THE WILD CHUTE

How did the shortest river in Texas become one of the state's most popular waterways?

The City Tube Chute helped make the gushing, spring-fed Comal River an irresistible attraction. Funneling across a dam in Prince Solms Park near downtown New Braunfels, the swirling chute helps send tube riders on a thrill ride on the Comal River. It starts a 2 1/2-hour float trip with an exhilarating rush. Sometimes it ends with a splash when the fast-flowing water overturns riders and their tubes. Summer is the busiest season, and it is the only time lifeguards are on duty. You can bypass the chute if you want to, but most swimmers can't resist the challenge.

For a little river, the Comal packs a punch. The springs that feed it gush 8 million gallons a minute and the water remains from 70-72 degrees year-round. It's considered the shortest navigable river in Texas. Ripley's Believe It Or Not once cited it as the shortest river in the United States, but that claim has been contested. Locals like to call it "the longest, shortest river." It flows for 2 ½ miles past downtown New Braunfels and Schlitterbahn Waterpark. The scenic channel is lined with towering cypress trees. The Spanish named it Comal, which means "flat dish," after the terrain that holds it. Early explorers first thought it was part of the Guadalupe, until it was identified as a separate river in 1727. It was one of the main reasons German settlers picked the townsite for New Braunfels.

Some of the denizens of the springs have been here long before the tourists came. The Comal is one of only two water

---

The City Tube Chute in New Braunfels starts a float trip on the Comal River with an exciting rush.

Left: *The shortest navigable river in Texas draws crowds of tubers.*

Right: *A float trip on the Comal River starts with a splash.*

sources in the world that supports minnow-sized, endangered fountain darters, Etheostoma fonticola. The tiny fish live near secondary springs in depths of three to five feet with water flow low enough to generate percolating sand that stirs up the invertebrates they feed on. It's the kind of habitat only found in the Comal and at the San Marcos springs in San Marcos. Stricter usage rules in recent years have aimed to conserve the fragile landscape for fish as well as people. Disposable drink containers and Styrofoam coolers, for example, are banned to slow down the litter that once spilled into the Comal, on purpose or by accident. Cell phones are permitted, but the City Tube Chute often wrenches them away, along with sunglasses and shoes. Just hold on tight and enjoy the ride.

SHORT AND SWEET

WHAT: City Tube Chute

WHERE: Prince Solms Park, 100 Liebscher Dr., New Braunfels, TX

COST: $5 for repeat rides, one-way is free.

PRO TIP: Tube rentals range from $15–$22, including shuttle pickup and drop-off. Rockin R' River Rides runs a popular, nearby service, (830) 620-6262. A list of others is available at tubeinnewbraunfels.com. For more information on the tube chute visit nbtexas.org/2579/comal-rive-info; or call (830) 221-4350.

NUTTY AND NICE

Where does some of the tastiest food in Texas fall from the sky?

When you drive a country road near San Saba, sometimes food does fall right out of the sky. It rains pecans. Dropped from overhanging limbs, nuts scatter across the pavement and crunch under your tires. No wonder San Saba calls itself the Pecan Capital of the World. There are eight commercial growers around the town. The harvest season runs from mid-October to late December.

E.E. Risien immigrated from England in 1874 and planted the roots of the industry when he developed improved varieties of native pecans that thrived along the San Saba River. His customers included Queen Victoria and cereal tycoon C.W. Post.

Risien's great-great-grandson, Winston Millican, runs Millican Pecan Company with his wife, Kristen. One of the family keepsakes they treasure is a fan letter from Alfred, Lord Tennyson. "We consider the walnut the best among our nuts...," the English poet wrote, "but to us your pecan nuts seem better still."

IN A NUTSHELL

WHAT: San Saba pecans

WHERE: Millican Pecan Company, 199 County Rd. 100; millicanpecancompany.com or (866) 484-6358.

COST: $2.80 for a pecan praline; $27.99 for a Texas pecan pie.

PRO TIP: Actor Tommy Lee Jones, sometimes seen around town, is a longtime local rancher.

San Saba grows pecans fit for royalty. Queen Victoria was once a customer. Every autumn, it rains nuts.

Top left: *Pecan trees frame the landmark courthouse in San Saba.*

Top inset: *The town calls itself the pecan capital of the world.*

Bottom left: *Millican Pecan Company, one of the oldest growers, once sold pecans to Queen Victoria.*

Bottom inset: *Pecan purveyors process the harvest from mid-October to late December.*

The Millicans grow 10 varieties of pecans on 1,000 acres. Their pecan company produces and sells dozens of pecan treats, from pies and preserves to pecan-flavored coffee. Another large grower, The Great San Saba River Pecan Company, has its store in a pecan orchard. One of its specialties, Pecan Pie-in-a-Jar ($19.95), holds all the fillings to make your own pecan pie. It's a treat even Queen Victoria might envy.

MONUMENTAL MOVE (page 106)

HISTORIC HARDWARE (page 38)

THE TOWN THE MAP FORGOT (page 36)

SECRET SWIMMING HOLE (page 110)

FALL FOR THE FRIO (page 178)
Photo courtesy of Texas Department of Parks and Wildlife

HEALING WATERS (page 62)

HAPPY HOUR AT THE P.O. (page 64)

WORLD CLASS SPUR (page 44)

HEADING FOR A HUNDRED (page 158)

QUIET PLEASE, CATTLE DRIVE PASSING THROUGH (page 82)

STAY A NIGHT ON TEDDY'S TRAIN (page 122)

TEXAS-SIZED CHRISTMAS ORNAMENT (page 66)
Photo courtesy of Fredericksburg Convention & Visitors Bureau

SECRETS OF THE DEEP (page 136)

STOPPING TIME AT THE FIVE AND DIME (page 138)

MUSIC AND A MEAL (page 160)

BETTER MILEAGE THAN A MULE (page 16)

MONUMENTAL MOVE

What mysterious forces left a copy of Stonehenge in a tiny Hill Country town?

Maybe the late Al Shepperd just liked to make people smile. No one knows exactly why he and his neighbor, Doug Hill, started building a mysterious monument beside the highway near Hunt, Texas. It started with a leftover block of stone. By the time they were finished in 1989, they created a near full-size copy of Stonehenge, the 5,000-year-old monument on Salisbury Plain in England. Hill added a couple of giant Easter Island heads for good measure. Passersby were startled and amused. A sign was added to the mystery. "Its purpose is unknown and perhaps unknowable," it read.

Locals got so used to Stonehenge II, they rallied when it was in danger of being torn down in 2010. The Hill Country Arts Foundation stepped in and raised funds to move the 75 pieces of the monument eight miles east to an honored site beside the Guadalupe River at the foundation's campus in Ingram. Visitors now get an up close look at the pieces that are 90 percent of the width of the original and 60 percent of the height. They are built on plaster and graphite-covered steel frames. The Easter Island heads, standing 13-feet-tall, are made of stone.

SET IN STONE

WHAT: Stonehenge II

WHERE: Hill Country Arts Foundation, 120 Point Theatre Rd., Ingram, TX

COST: Free

PRO TIP: The Hill Country Arts Foundation holds year-round art shows and performances. The Hill Country Celtic Festival, held in early October, features Highland games and dancing; hcaf.com; (830) 367-5121.

Top: *The town of Ingram has a Stonehenge of its own.*

Inset: *Giant Easter Island heads keep watch.*

Not long after it was moved, Stonehenge II appeared as a backdrop for one of the early episodes of *Friday Night Lights*. It isn't oriented toward the sun like the original, but it does have an upcoming date with the earth's closest star. It sits directly in the path of the April 8, 2024 solar eclipse. For 4 minutes and 26 seconds, there will be even less light than there usually is on the magical mystery of Stonehenge II.

You don't have to cross the ocean to catch a vision of one of England's oldest marvels.

FINDING MIRACLES IN UTOPIA

Can a visit to a picturesque tiny town change your life and fix your golf swing?

Settlers were going to call the town "Montana" because of the beautiful scenery that surrounds it, but George Barker had a better idea. Barker was ailing—possibly from tuberculosis—when he arrived to serve as a school teacher and the first postmaster. To try to regain his health, he swam every morning in the crystal-clear, spring-fed Sabinal River. According to local lore, Barker was cured. He suggested a new name—Utopia, because it "was a perfect place to be," says local historian Diane Causey.

With no traffic lights, a population of 360, and a bucolic Main Street, Utopia is still pretty much a perfect place to be. Visitors can still swim in the refreshing waters of Utopia Park Lake Dam. They join locals for lunch at Lost Maples Café and drive winding roads that glow in autumn with crimson colors of bigtooth maples, red oaks, Texas cherry, and flame sumac.

Golf is one of Utopia's most recent miracles. The town was the setting for Dr. David Cook's

A PERFECT PLACE

WHAT: Utopia

WHERE: Ranch Rd. 187, about a 90-minute drive northwest of San Antonio

COST: Daily admission fee for swimmers is $10 per person at Utopia Park Lake Dam, visit utopiapark.org, or call (830) 966-3643. For tee times at the Links of Utopia, call (830) 966-5577.

PRO TIP: Even though it is off the beaten path, Utopia is a gateway to popular Lost Maples State Natural Area. It draws its biggest crowds at the start of the fall color season in late October. Summers are slower. The hour-long fireworks show at Lake Dam Park is a nice way to enjoy a small town July Fourth celebration.

Top: *Utopia Park Lake is a refreshing oasis on a hot day.*

Inset: *Utopia treasures its place of beauty in the Hill Country.*

inspirational book, *Golf's Sacred Journey,* and it was the location for the 2011 film, *Seven Days in Utopia,* starring Robert Duvall and Lucas Black. Duvall helped Black's character get his game back. "I think there's something here that everyone is looking for," says Dr. Cook. Golfers come from all over the country to make a pilgrimage to the nine-hole Links of Utopia.

Utopia might not change your life or cure your golf slice, but it's worth a shot.

SECRET SWIMMING HOLE

Where can you find an old-fashioned swimming hole with unspoiled natural beauty?

Try Krause Springs. Most people are surprised to discover this hidden gem when they first see it. Shaded by towering cypress trees and watered by more than 30 springs, it's an oasis like no other on a hot summer day. Go ahead. Grab the rope swing. Jump in. Be a kid again.

Krause Springs is a throwback to simpler times. It looks like a piece of fairytale fantasy that Disney might spend a fortune to create. Only this one is real. Nature made it. Nature and Elton Krause. He and his wife, Jane, bought Krause Springs from an aunt in 1955. Elton knew what a wonder it was. He grew up in Spicewood, three miles away. Elton labored to build many of the trails that lead down to the spring-fed pool in Cypress Creek. He added gardens, campgrounds, and a spring-fed swimming pool.

STAYING COOL

WHAT: Krause Springs

WHERE: 424 County Rd. 404, Spicewood, TX

COST: $8 adults, $5 ages 4–11

PRO TIP: The water stays a constant 70 degrees, and unlike some other swimming areas in the Hill Country, even the driest weather has never stopped the springs' flow.

Less than an hour's drive from Austin, Krause Springs is a hidden oasis that's one of the Hill Country's best swimming holes.

Top: *Krause Springs is a hidden oasis.*

Inset: *A waterfall tumbles into the spring-fed pool.*

Photos courtesy of Krause Springs

In springtime, butterflies attracted by Elton's flower gardens float among the ancient cypress trees that shade the springs. Elton passed away in 2011 at the age of 88, and Jane preceded him, but the couple left an oasis that's often called one of the state's best swimming holes. It's still operated by the Krause family as it has been for more than 50 years.

LLANO ROCKS

Where can you find one of the rarest rocks in the world?

Ask the bartender. Or better yet just look down at the long slab of sparkling stone beneath your drink on the bar at the historic Badu 1891 restaurant in Llano. It's made with the longest section of llanite in the world. In Llano, set in the center of an area filled with unusual rocks and minerals, llanite is one of the rarest. Llano is said to be the only place in the world where it is found.

The Llano Uplift, a rise of mostly granite rock that stretches for almost 50 miles along Texas 29, is a weathered remnant of the Precambrian age that forms the town's most prominent stony landmark. The area is a mother lode for rock hounds. Collectors find smoky quartz, galena, and even traces of gold in the Llano River. One of the rarest is llanite, a type of granite flecked with blue quartz crystals.

Enchanted Rocks & Jewelry on the square is stuffed with prized examples of local rocks. Owner

SOLID AS A ROCK

WHAT: Llanite

WHERE: Found around Llano and nowhere else in the world. The bar at the Badu 1891 restaurant is made of it.

COST: Price of a drink at the Badu 1891, at 801 Bessemer Ave., Llano, TX. Open for dinner Wednesday–Saturday, lunch on Saturday, and brunch on Sunday; badu1891.com. Enchanted Rocks & Jewelry opens on Friday and Saturday noon to 5 p.m.; (325) 247-4137.

PRO TIP: Don't miss the brisket, beef ribs, and sausage cooked over outdoor pits at Cooper's Old Time Pit Bar-B-Que in Llano. It gets crowded at lunch and dinner, but it serves some of the most delicious barbecue in the state.

Llano is a paradise for rock hounds. The cool clear waters of the Llano River sometimes yield a flash of gold.

Top: *A popular local shop helps rockhounds identify their finds in Llano.*

Inset: *Llano is said to be the only place in the world where llanite is found.*

Bottom: *The area is a mother lode of unusual rocks and minerals.*

Frank Rowell and his wife, Patricia Felts, identify visitors' finds and direct them to likely places to look. One of the favorites is the Llano river bed, where floods often leave sought-after rocks in gravel deposits near water crossings and along the banks. "It's a treasure hunt anyone can go on," Patricia told *Texas Highways Magazine* in 2020. "You don't need high-tech equipment. You don't have to be rich. You don't have to go to some exotic location. There are rocks everywhere."

LODGE IN A LANDMARK

Would you consider a tiny room without television, a phone, or room service a refreshing experience?

The Landmark Inn in Castroville has been hosting travelers since 1853. When I checked in, my room was up a set of outdoor stairs in a weathered, two-story outbuilding. The downstairs was once a bathhouse, the only man-made bath between San Antonio and Eagle Pass. The ceilings were so low, I had to bend down to look in the bathroom mirror. There was a brass bed, but not much else. As a travel editor at *Southern Living Magazine* for many years, I often stayed in some of the most luxurious hotels and resorts in the country. I thought the bathhouse tower room might be the worst place I ever spent the night—then I opened the guest book of memories on a table by the bed. What I read taught me that you don't need a grand hotel to have a grand experience.

One woman wrote about the enchantment she felt at a simple wedding, held on the grounds of the inn beside the Medina River. Guests gave her bouquets of wildflowers. The tiny tower room

ROOMS AT THE INN

WHAT: Landmark Inn State Historic Site Bed and Breakfast

WHERE: 402 E Florence St., Castroville, TX

COST: Room rates start at $120 per night. For reservations, call (830) 931-2133 or email landmarkinnstaff@thc.texas.gov.

PRO TIP: If you can't stay the night, guided tours give visitors a look at the hotel and grounds, including the bathhouse. Cost is $4 adults, $3 seniors and ages 3–16. For reservations, call (830) 931-2133.

Travelers take a step back in time when they stay at the Landmark Inn.

Left: *The bathhouse tower room is a relic of frontier days when the inn offered the only bath between San Antonio and Eagle Pass.*

Right: *The Landmark Inn is preserved in Castroville.*

Inset: *It operates now as a state historic site bed and breakfast.*

was her honeymoon suite. She said she would always remember it. Another couple wrote about the comfort they felt in the coziness of the little room. They had just reunited with their son, a soldier. He was safe, home from Iraq. In entry after entry, that little book taught me how much a travel experience can mean to people. It taught me to be a little less spoiled. It taught me that sharing time with others can sometimes mean more than a plush place to stay.

The Landmark Inn isn't able to use the room above the bathhouse now—the stairs became too shaky, and there were other safety issues, but there are eight other rustic little rooms. No televisions. No room service. No one would ever call them plush or luxurious. But if you get the chance, try one sometime. You might just make a memory.

ON THIS CAMPUS, A RIVER RUNS THROUGH IT

Why do students at Texas State University jump in the river when they graduate?

Because they love it. The spring-fed San Marcos River has been a cherished part of the San Marcos campus ever since math professor S.M. "Froggy" Sewell went wading in it on a hot summer day in 1916. The water was only three feet deep and the banks were choked with weeds. Dr. Sewell decided the university needed a better swimming hole. He set in motion improvements that eventually made the spring-fed river a centerpiece of the school. It was called Riverside Park until 1946 when it was renamed Sewell Park in his honor.

At a constant 72 degrees year-round, the river is a popular place for tubing, sunbathing, picnicking—and even a little studying. It's so steeped in campus tradition, class rings include an image of tubes floating past Old Main, the school's first major building. Continuing other long-standing traditions, students dip their rings in the nearby

---

SPRING BREAK

WHAT: Sewell Park

WHERE: 700-1 Aquarena Springs Dr. on the Texas State University campus

COST: Free, but hours vary and reservations may be required due to Covid-19 restrictions. Call (512) 245-2004, or visit campusrecreation.txstate.edu.

PRO TIP: Take an hour-long tube ride on the river at nearby San Marcos City Park. Lions Club Tube Rental distributes tubes there and operates shuttles to pick up tubers at Rio Vista Park. Cost is $16 with a tube, and $10 if you bring your own. Reservations are required and hours may vary because of Covid-19 restrictions; visit tubesanmarcos.com for reservations.

Top: *The San Marcos River is a beloved part of the Texas State University campus.*

Bottom: *Between classes the river is a respite for students.*

headwaters of the river soon after they get them. After they graduate, many rush to the river in caps and gowns and leap in.

The river isn't the only water that graces the campus. A decade before the university opened in 1903, fish schooled the grounds at the oldest warm-water US Federal Fish Hatchery west of the Mississippi River. After the fishery closed in 1965, the 43-acre facility was turned over to the university. It united the campus and provided space for future growth. The former fish ponds surround the Theatre Center and J.C. Kellam Administration Building. They are used by Texas State's Aquatic Biology Program.

Texas State University is a beautiful campus to take a walk—or a swim.

SAVED BY A HAIR

Where can you get a shave and a haircut in a barber shop so old it's a museum?

You won't find a sports channel or even a television blaring in the Buck Horn Barbershop in New Braunfels. It doesn't need all that. Melissa Epps keeps customers entertained with almost everything they need to know about the picturesque town with a vintage barbershop that's been in business since 1920.

"I'm the third barber who's worked here in the 101 years it's been in business," she says proudly. Oscar Wagenfuehr and his son Fred, the two barbers that preceeded Melissa, left plenty behind to remember them by as well. They spent lifetimes cutting hair and meticulously building the handcrafted circus wagons, acrobats, clowns, and animals that fill display cases at the shop. When Fred passed, he willed the barbershop and the family home next to it to the New Braunfels Conservation Society. The Conservation Society operates the home as a bed and breakfast. The barbershop is preserved as a museum, but it's also still a good place to get a haircut. (Melissa was a recent winner of the local newspaper's readers' choice award for the town's best barber.)

Almost everything in the shop, the chairs and free-standing sink that dispenses steaming water for shaves, is just as the

SHAVE AND A HAIRCUT

WHAT: Wagenfuehr Buck Horn Barbershop

WHERE: 521 W San Antonio St., New Braunfels, TX

COST: $18 for a haircut. Tours are free, but donations are appreciated.

PRO TIP: Call for an appointment, (830) 629-2943. Melissa is at the shop 9:30 a.m. to 5 p.m. Tuesday–Friday, and mornings on Saturday. Wagenfuehr Bed and Breakfast next door is a good location for exploring the downtown historic district. For reservations and more information, contact the New Braunfels Conservation Society; (830) 832-7543.

Top: *Buck Horn Barber Shop is both a museum and an operating barbershop.*

Inset: *Vintage chairs decorate the shop that opened in 1920.*

Wagenfuerhrs' left it. Shaves are given with a strait edge razor and a hot towel. Melissa set out to become a beautician, but decided she liked cutting men's hair better. "I went to beauty school and lasted three days," she recalls. "Then I went to barber college and just loved it."

She said men can hold their own when it comes to telling tales. "I found that men are just as bad as women when it comes to gossiping," she says.

Opened more than a century ago, one of the oldest barbershops in Texas is still clipping along in New Braunfels.

SOME SMALL WONDERS IN LUCKENBACH

Who was the joker who invented the most famous tiny town in America?

PUT ON YOUR BOOTS AND FADED JEANS

WHAT: Luckenbach General Store and dance hall

WHERE: 412 Luckenbach Loop. From Fredericksburg, go six miles east on US 290, turn right on Ranch Road 1376 for 4.6 miles and turn right on the Luckenbach Town Loop.

COST: Admission to the general store and grounds is free, unless there's a special event.

PRO TIP: Sip a cold drink and listen to music on the outdoor stage. Try your hand at washer pitching. If you get there early in the day, Luckenbach is almost as relaxing as it was when Hondo bought it. It livens up when the dance hall hosts live performances. For schedules, visit luckenbach.com, or call 1-888-997-3224.

If you wonder who put the magic in Luckenbach, you can thank a man named John Russell Crouch. Everyone called him "Hondo." His bronze bust stands outside the battered and rusty-roofed Luckenbach General Store. Dressed in a stained and wrinkled straw hat, knee-high boots, and an ever-present red bandana beneath his bushy white beard, Hondo was a hypnotizing presence.

He and Guich Koock bought the end-of-nowhere town in 1971 and Hondo set to work reinventing it. When asked why he bought the town, Hondo simply explained "Dallas wasn't for sale—besides the American way is to start small and work your way up." He believed Luckenbach was the center of the world, and proved it with a globe. He put a piece of string on Luckenbach, stretched it around the globe, and "danged if the other end didn't fall on Luckenbach too."

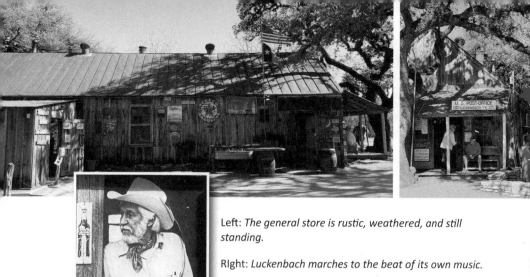

Left: *The general store is rustic, weathered, and still standing.*

Right: *Luckenbach marches to the beat of its own music.*

Inset: *Hondo Crouch brought the world to Luckenbach.*

He coined the welcome that became the state's most popular bumper sticker, "Everybody's Somebody in Luckenbach." He made up celebrations like the "Non-buy Centennial" and the "Return of the Mud Dobbers" festival.

Hondo passed away peacefully in 1976. A year later, the Waylon Jennings classic, "Luckenbach, Texas," made the town a place where thousands of listeners longed to "get back to the basics in life." Hondo had a gift for seeing the small wonders and miracles in life that most people look right past. He talked about that in his poem, "Luckenbach Daylight. A Luckenbach daylight is that time of day you wish would never go away…"

Hondo Crouch proved that sometimes good things come in small packages.

STAY A NIGHT ON TEDDY'S TRAIN

How did America's most famous Rough Rider travel in comfort when he visited Texas?

Guests can make themselves at home in all sorts of comfortable lodging places in Fredericksburg, but few can carry you back in time like the handsome 1894 Private Palace Pullman Car that sits a few blocks from the town's historic Main Street. Step inside and you'll find photographs, furnishings, and keepsakes that honor the elegant car's most famous lodger, President Teddy Roosevelt.

Now restored for overnight guests, the car was used by Roosevelt when he visited Texas shortly after he was inaugurated in 1905. He attended a reunion of the Rough Riders in San Antonio and then traveled to Fort Worth to go on a wolf hunt in Oklahoma organized by rancher Burk Burnett, owner of the legendary 6666 Ranch. To travel to the hunt, Burnett supplied

ALL ABOARD

WHAT: 1894 Private Palace Pullman Car

WHERE: 431 S Lincoln St., Fredericksburg, TX

COST: Rates start at $265 per night, limited to two people and there is a two-night minimum on weekends; fredericksburgescapes.com, or (888) 991-6749.

PRO TIP: It's a fairly steep climb up the car's steps and hallways are tight, so it may not be possible to access if your mobility is limited.

A Pullman car that once carried Teddy Roosevelt on a wolf hunt now gives Hill Country visitors an enchanting place to spend the night.

Right: *Teddy Roosevelt traveled Texas in his private Pullman car.*

Left: *A Presidential Seal honors the elegant car's most famous lodger.*

Bottom: *Memorabilia decorates the train car that is now used as a bed and breakfast.*

his private Pullman car, specially built for his friend, Comanche Chief Quanah Parker's, Quanah, Acme & Pacific Railroad. Burnett and Parker hosted the hunt, held in the Big Pasture leased by Burnett on Comanche lands, north of the Red River. The hunt featured Jack Abernathy, an outdoorsman who could catch wolves barehanded. Roosevelt was enthralled. He wrote to his son, Ted, that the hunt brought in "17 wolves, three coons, and any number of rattlesnakes."

Photographs, letters, paintings, and other items documenting the trip decorate the Pullman car. Guests relax in a set of rooms that includes a kitchen, bedroom, and sitting room. The car is co-owned by Mark Wieser and Case Fischer, who also operate the nearby Fischer & Wieser Food Products. The Pullman was often used by visiting chefs before it was opened to the public. After it was restored, Mark, a history buff, searched for and purchased the memorabilia used to furnish it.

THE CAPTAIN'S MANSION

How did a man who walked to Kerrville to save money, build one of Texas's biggest empires?

They say Charles Schreiner walked to Kerrville when he first came to town to save stagecoach fare. That's one of the Schreiner legends. There are many. He also helped start the college that became Schreiner University, even though he had very little formal education himself. He built one of the state's most famous stores, started a bank, an electric company, and dozens of other enterprises. In his spare time, he was a Texas Ranger and a cattle baron. With profits from driving more than 300,000 head up the trail to Kansas, he bought the legendary YO Ranch and grew it into one of the largest spreads in Texas, covering more than 600,000 acres.

His also built the castle-like Schreiner Mansion that's preserved in downtown Kerrville as a museum that showcases the captain's legacy. Schreiner didn't shower many luxuries on himself, but the elegant mansion is an exception. He hired the Hill Country's most respected architect, Alfred Giles, to design it. Giles added turrets reminiscent of the castle in the Alsatian region of France where Schreiner's father was born before the family immigrated to San Antonio. After his father's death, Schreiner took over responsibility for his mother and siblings. He was only 14, but he was soon on the path of storekeeping, banking, and business-building that made him a sort of J.P. Morgan of the Hill Country.

His first thriving business in Kerrville was the Schreiner General Store. The first frame store originally stood next door to the mansion. Tradition holds that it was connected to the mansion by a tunnel, so Schreiner could bring home the day's receipts without risking bandits on the street of the frontier town. He and his family lived in the backroom of the store for eight years while they waited for the mansion to be finished. Stone masons, brought from Germany, crafted its stately

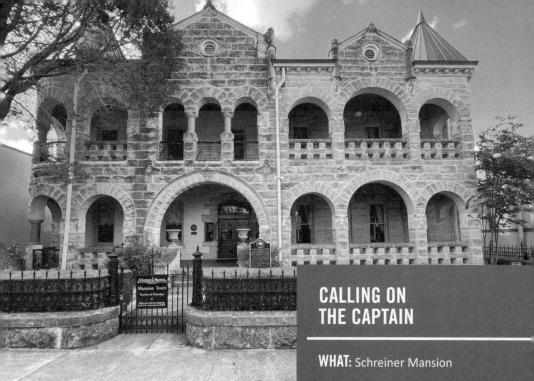

Charles Schreiner's elegant mansion is preserved in Kerrville where he began his ranching empire.

limestone exterior. The elegant interior was illuminated with the town's first electric lights. In the front yard, there's a spreading pinon tree, said to have grown from a seed brought back from New Mexico after a cattle drive. In many ways, Captain Schreiner planted the seeds that grew the whole town.

CALLING ON THE CAPTAIN

WHAT: Schreiner Mansion

WHERE: 226 Earl Garrett St., Kerrville, TX

COST: $7 adults, $5 students for tours offered on Tuesdays and Thursdays from 10 a.m. to 2 p.m. Visit caillouxfoundation.org/schreiner-mansion; or call (830) 895-5222.

PRO TIP: The nearby Schreiner Department Store operated until 2007. Now the building houses other businesses, including Schreiner Goods, a women's fashions boutique at 214 Earl Garret Street.

How did a 14-year-old boy with hardly any formal education grow up to become the J.P. Morgan of the Hill Country?

THE HILL COUNTRY'S BEST OLD CURIOSITY STOP

Where can you see a well-dressed flea or a two-headed lamb?

In addition to publishing a magazine that saved some of the best first-person accounts of Texas history on record, J. Marvin Hunter's curiosity knew no bounds. He often said he didn't collect rarities, but rarities collected him. His stash fills the Frontier Times Museum in Bandera. When you step inside, you realize it's the kind of place where you expected to spend five minutes, and you wind up browsing around for the whole afternoon. One rarity leads to another, like a treasure hunt, with 40,000 artifacts. Some of it is just plain odd, like the dressed fleas that can be viewed under a microscope, or a two-headed lamb, or the birthing chair from the Middle Ages.

"The building itself is an artifact," points out Executive Director Rebecca Norton. "It's made out of native limestone and within the walls you have petrified wood, fossilized coral and various crystals. The museum is a traditional cabinet of curiosity, with eclectic collections that speak to Bandera County and life on the Texas Frontier."

Hunter opened the museum in 1933 to help promote his *Frontier Times Magazine* and bring tourism to Bandera. Reprints

Editor and historian J. Marvin Hunter spent a lifetime collecting stories and keepsakes of the frontier for his museum in Bandera.

Left: *Historian and publisher J. Marvin Hunter built the Frontier Times Museum in Bandera.*

Right: *The museum features more than 40,000 artifacts.*

of the magazine, published from 1923 to 1954, are available in the museum and online.

The museum's founder tracked down colorful characters all over the West. The many books he published include the autobiography of gunslinger John Wesley Hardin. He edited *The Trail Drivers of Texas*, filled with first-person accounts. In addition to all his other work, he operated more than 16 newspapers in his lifetime, including the *Bandera Bulletin* up until his death in 1957.

HUNTER AND GATHERER

WHAT: Frontier Times Museum

WHERE: 510 13th St., Bandera, TX; 10 a.m. to 4:30 p.m. Monday–Saturday, closed Sundays, except for special programs.

COST: Adults, $6, seniors, $4, children 6–12, $2.

PRO TIP: The museum periodically hosts the Frontier Times Jamboree on the 4th Sunday of the month, with free admission, music and storytelling from 1–4 p.m. For information, visitfrontiertimesmuseum.org, or call (830) 796-3864. For information on copies of *Frontier Times Magazine*, visit frontiertimesmagazine.com.

THIS OLD HOUSE CROSSED THE OCEAN

Where can you see a nearly four-century-old French house that now lives in Texas?

European settlers have been coming to the Hill Country since the early 19th century. But in Castroville, a whole house migrated.

It took four years to painstakingly reconstruct the Steinbach House, after it was shipped to Texas in 1998 as a gift from the Alsatian people. The two-story timber and stone dwelling serves as a visitor center and museum in Castroville, a town started by European settlers from the Alsace region on the border between France and Germany.

The Steinbach House was built between 1618 and 1648 in Wahlbach, France. The framework was disassembled, shipped to Houston, and sent to Castroville by truck. Craftsmen from Alsace, France helped reconstruct it. It was finished with doors, windows, and shutters made in France.

HOME PLACE

WHAT: Steinbach House

WHERE: 203 US 290, Castroville, TX

COST: Free. Tours are offered 10 a.m. to 4 p.m. Thursday–Saturday and 11 a.m. to 3 p.m. Sunday; steinbachhouse.org; (830) 538-9838.

PRO TIP: If you get there early, don't miss the donuts and pastries at nearby Haby's Alsatian Bakery, 207 US 290 East, (830) 538-2718. It opens at 5:30 a.m. Monday–Saturday, closed on Sunday.

The oldest house in Castroville is a long, long way from home.

Top: *The farm wagon and other exhibits depict the Alsatian way of life.*

Inset: *Built in the 17th century, the house was reassembled by old world craftsmen as a gift to the town.*

Bottom: *The Steinbach House was shipped to Castroville from the Alsace region of France where many of the town's settlers originated.*

The Steinbach House is the oldest building in a town that has done much to maintain its distinctive Alsatian heritage. On walking tours, visitors can see 97 historic buildings, ranging from modest homes to imposing landmarks such as the St. Louis Catholic Church and Zion Lutheran Church. Now sitting in a place of honor, the Steinbach House is a great place to start.

THE HOLE
OF NO RETURN

Just who is at the bottom of Dead Man's Hole?

No one knows for sure. Maybe a judge was thrown in. And 20 or 30 others. No one was keeping score. Or records. The fire eaters knew. It was the place where they made their enemies disappear in the rowdy days when Burnet County split its loyalties between the North and South.

In a lonesome rocky field south of Marble Falls, Dead Man's Hole was left to hold its secrets. Ferdinand Lueders, a German entomologist hunting for night-flying insects, stumbled across its entrance in 1821. It didn't become handy for more sinister uses until the start of the Civil War. It seemed bottomless. Toxic gases kept out nosey intruders. No one even knew how deep it was until a pair of University of Texas spelunkers explored it using breathing equipment in 1951. They pegged it at just over 15 stories deep. By then, any evidence at the bottom had long since disappeared.

GOOD TILL THE LAST DROP

WHAT: Dead Man's Hole

WHERE: County Rd. 401, Marble Falls, TX

COST: Free

PRO TIP: The park is tricky to find on Google maps. To reach it, take US 281 south from Marble Falls, turn east on Farm Road 2147 for one-half mile and go south for one mile on County Road 401 to a small street sign that says "Dead Man's Hole."

A deep dark hole near Marble Falls is filled with mysteries. No one knows how many lost souls disappeared in it.

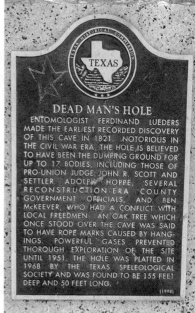

DEAD MAN'S HOLE
ENTOMOLOGIST FERDINAND LUEDERS MADE THE EARLIEST RECORDED DISCOVERY OF THIS CAVE IN 1821. NOTORIOUS IN THE CIVIL WAR ERA, THE HOLE IS BELIEVED TO HAVE BEEN THE DUMPING GROUND FOR UP TO 17 BODIES, INCLUDING THOSE OF PRO-UNION JUDGE JOHN R. SCOTT AND SETTLER ADOLPH HOPPE, SEVERAL RECONSTRUCTION-ERA COUNTY GOVERNMENT OFFICIALS, AND BEN McKEEVER, WHO HAD A CONFLICT WITH LOCAL FREEDMEN. AN OAK TREE WHICH ONCE STOOD OVER THE CAVE WAS SAID TO HAVE ROPE MARKS CAUSED BY HANGINGS. POWERFUL GASES PREVENTED THOROUGH EXPLORATION OF THE SITE UNTIL 1951. THE HOLE WAS PLATTED IN 1968 BY THE TEXAS SPELEOLOGICAL SOCIETY AND WAS FOUND TO BE 155 FEET DEEP AND 50 FEET LONG.

(1998)

Left: *Now sealed off, a bottomless pit was a final resting place for as many as 30 lost souls.*

Right: *A marker records the history of the infamous landmark discovered in 1821.*

Inset: *The mysteries linger on at Dead Man's Hole.*

But the mysteries linger on. County Judge John R. Scott was the most famous person said to have taken the drop. He was pro Union, even though he had four sons in the Confederate army. The pro-South vigilantes, known as fire eaters, wanted him gone. He soon dropped out of sight. So did other pro-Union sympathizers. Some say it was 17. Or as many as 36.

The 6 ½ acres around Dead Man's Hole is a county park now. The hole has a cover over it to protect visitors from falling in. Local lore contends that you can sometimes hear strange voices there at night. Perhaps someone just wants to have the last word.

SAVING THE SHOW

How did New Braunfels keep the last picture show from having a bad ending?

It took a lot of hard work. The Brauntex Theatre was headed for the wrecking ball when it closed in 1998. Seats were torn and faded. Curtains were frayed and almost everything else in the building was in disrepair. So many letters had fallen off its San Antonio street sign, locals began calling it the Brau.

Demolition was imminent when local performing arts groups and other volunteers stepped in to save it. One group of women, who called themselves the Brauntex Sweatshop, sewed more than 600 seat covers. Gradually the landmark was put back in shape. It now hosts year-round performances—concerts, musicals, touring stars, plays, and other events.

The interior is even grander than it was when the Brauntex opened on January 6, 1942, a month after Pearl Harbor was attacked. Projectionist Walter Braune sparked up the rectifiers in the projector to screen *Birth of the Blues*, starring Bing Crosby and Texas native Mary Martin. Tickets cost 30 cents. During World War II, the theater screened news reels and audiences watched as G.I.'s slugged their way across North Africa, Europe, and the Pacific Islands.

In the decades that followed, the Brauntex tried its best to keep up with the changing times. In one effort to add more patrons, the balcony was enclosed in 1972 to hold a "mini" theater. The Brauntex operated as a dual cinema until it closed

The Art Deco Brauntex Theatre, restored and listed on the National Register of Historic Places, is enjoying an encore as a performance hall.

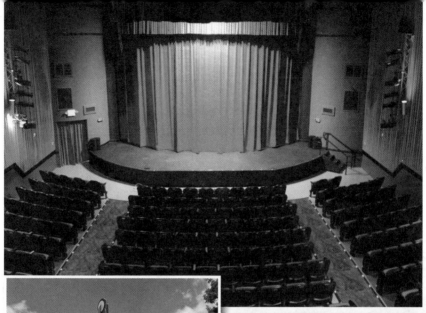

Top: *The Brauntex Theatre elegant performance hall hosts a variety of shows year-round.*

Inset: *The now restored theater opened in 1942 a month after Pearl Harbor.*

BOX OFFICE

WHAT: Brauntex Theatre

WHERE: 290 W San Antonio, New Braunfels, TX

COST: Ticket prices vary. For show schedules, visit brauntex.org or call (830) 627-0808.

PRO TIP: The theater is celebrating its 80th birthday in 2022. Watch for special events.

in 1998. The renovations brought back the balcony to enlarge capacity to 584 seats. The stage was also expanded to make room for larger performances. In 2008, the Brauntex became one of the few preserved movie theaters in the state to be included on the National Register of Historic Places. Outfitted with plush red seats and royal red curtains, the 80-year-old landmark provides a comfortable and intimate setting to see a performance. It's an especially cozy place to sit back and enjoy some of the music stars who perform there regularly.

HONKY-TONK MAN

Where can you two-step across one of the oldest honky-tonks in Texas?

No one is even sure where the name "honky-tonk" came from. Some say it's what cowboys called a rowdy saloon. Others believe it was coined from the way boisterous music sounded when it boomed out the door of a bar. The songs were mostly sorrowful—stories of things lost, or never found. A writer for the Grand Ole Opry once described it as a place where "the beer is cold, the music is good, and…the artists who take the stage are all chasing a dream."

Arkey Blue would qualify. So would Arkey Blue's Silver Dollar, the honky-tonk he took over in 1968, and where he still takes the stage every Saturday night. The Silver Dollar ought to be in the dictionary under "honky-tonk," in case anyone wonders what one looks like.

Even on a sunlight afternoon, it's as dark as a cave. You enter through a red door on Main Street in Bandera beside the general store and step down a flight of stairs. Neon signs light the way to the bar in back. To the right is a small stage. Most of the regulars are dressed in boots and hats in a town that calls itself "The Cowboy Capital of the World."

BANDERA BALLADS

WHAT: Arkey Blue's Silver Dollar

WHERE: 308 Main St., Bandera, TX

COST: $5 cover on Saturday nights when Arkey Blue and the Blue Cowboys Play

PRO TIP: "Backstreets of Bandera," "Whiskey in Your Eyes," and many of Arkey's other songs can be heard on YouTube.

The music plays on at Arkey Blue's Silver Dollar in the Cowboy Capital of the World.

Top: *The music plays on at Arkey Blue's Silver Dollar.*

Inset: *A painting and other mementos honor the saloon's namesake.*

Bottom: *Neon signs light the way.*

"That's not sawdust on the floor," Arkey likes to joke when he sees a new face. "It's last night's furniture." Arkey Juenke became Arkey Blue after a record producer noticed he had a penchant for singing blue, sad songs. Before moving on to a stage of his own, he started his musical career playing his guitar and singing for guests at a Bandera dude ranch, where he worked days as a wrangler. He's written enough songs to fill an outline of the state of Texas that hangs on a wall at the Silver Dollar.

Arkey is a treasured icon in Bandera, where he has been inducted into the Bandera Music Hall of Fame as a Living Legend. The big spotlight of country music fame has yet to shine his way, but no matter. Dreams are made to be chased. That's what honky-tonks are for.

SECRETS OF THE DEEP

What makes Jacob's Well so beautiful and so deadly?

Gaze down into the crystal clear depths of Jacob's Well and it's easy to see why so many have been charmed by its beauty.

Beneath a circular, 12-feet-wide opening, the waters seem bottomless. Swimmers come to splash in the chilly, 68-degree, spring-fed oasis near Wimberley year-round. But for some, the mysterious depths have held a fatal attraction. At least eight scuba divers—and some say as many as 12—have perished in the dark recesses of the cave that meanders far below the surface.

So many were lost, metal bars were put in place below the lower cave entrance to keep divers from entering the depths and diving was prohibited. The main opening goes down 23 feet, then angles off to a final depth of 137 feet. Cramped passages lead off to a larger cave that meanders for almost a mile far below the surface. A smaller cave extends another 1,300 feet. The cave floors are covered in silt and deep, unstable gravel that makes them even more treacherous. Several of the lost were experienced divers. It's believed that some were afflicted with nitrogen narcosis, a condition that causes divers to lose direction and become confused and disoriented.

MYSTERIOUS PLACE

WHAT: Jacob's Well Natural Area

WHERE: 1699 Mt. Sharpe Rd., Wimberley, TX

COST: Admission to the natural area is free. Cost for swimming is $9 adults, $5 children. Numbers of swimmers are limited, and reservations are required; visit parks@co.hays.tx.us, or call (512) 214-4593.

PRO TIP: Be sure to bring water, the natural area doesn't have water fountains. It's about a 15-minute walk from the parking area to Jacob's Well. Naturalists lead hour-long guided hikes at 9 a.m. on the second and fourth Saturdays each month, except during the summer. Reservations are required; parks@co.hays.tx.us, or call (512) 214-4593.

Top: *Springs feed a pool that extends for more than a mile below the surface.*

Inset: *A swimmer takes a leap at Jacob's Well.*

In earlier times, the springs gushed with such force that it was almost impossible for swimmers to drown. The flow pushed them back to the surface. Ironically, the oasis that lured so many to their deaths, has been in danger of dying itself. The flow stopped—for the first time in recorded history—in 2000, and again in 2008, and 2011. Efforts since have tried to protect water sources and 82-acres around Jacob's Well is set aside as a natural area where visitors come for hiking, swimming, and nature tours.

At least eight divers have perished in the mysterious waters of Jacob's Well, one of the most lethal underwater caves in America. Diving is now prohibited.

STOPPING TIME AT THE FIVE AND DIME

Need a gadget to measure a "nip" or a "smidgeon," or a bottle of perfume from the Thirties?

Dooley's 5-10-25 Cent Store is your place. Opened in 1923, the store is one of the last of the old-time Five and Dimers in America. Rows of shelves are piled high with pickle crocks, toy tractors, balsam wood airplanes, and kitchen gadgets that look like they belong in another century. Some of them do. Owner Tim Dooley still stocks some of the items his grandfather sold when he opened the store.

A walk down the aisles feels more like a treasure hunt than a shopping trip. It's one of the last places in the United States to find Blue Waltz perfume, a fragrance popular in the 1930s. "It's what your grandmother wore," Tim says. The rest of the inventory hasn't changed much either. "We've been buying from the same supplier for 40 years," Tim explains.

A STORE AND MORE

WHAT: Dooley's 5-10-25 Cent Store

WHERE: 131 E Main St., Fredericksburg, TX

COST: A bottle of Blue Waltz perfume will set you back $3.99. A "smidgeon" measuring device runs $4.49.

PRO TIP: Dooley's doesn't take credit or debit cards, but it has an ATM machine. Mail order information is available at dooleys5-10@austin.rr.com; or (830) 997-3458.

Almost a century old, Dooley's 5-10-25 Cent Store is one of the last remaining Five and Dime stores in America.

Top: *Dooley's 5-10-25 cent Store has been a fixture on Main Street in Fredericksburg for nearly a century.*

Left inset: *You can find measuring spoons for a "nip" or a "smidgen."*

Right inset: *The store offers one of the last stocks of Blue Waltz perfume popular in the 1930s.*

Bottom: *Owner Tim Dooley's crazy hat section fills one aisle.*

Household supplies include a sprinkler cap you can plug in the top of a soft drink bottle filled with water to dampen ironing and long-handled mops made for applying barbecue sauce on a grill. One gadget is set up to measure a "nip," "smidgeon," or "dash."

The toy section is a throwback to simpler times too. You won't find any video games, but there's a nice selection of toy tractors and other aluminum farm toys. Small balsam wood glider airplanes are popular too.

What Tim calls his "crazy hat" section fills another aisle. One of the favorites is a pink cowgirl hat that lights up. If you need something a little more formal, there are crowns and scepters too. Crown yourself if you feel like it. At Dooley's it doesn't cost much to have a royal experience.

TUNNEL VISION

Why do dozens of visitors show up at sunset to look inside an abandoned railroad tunnel near Fredericksburg?

They aren't waiting for a train. The last one pulled out of Fredericksburg on its way to San Antonio in the 1940s, but the deep dark passageway—the length of three football fields—was perfect for millions of new inhabitants who moved in after the trains left. The tunnel is now home to a huge colony of Mexican free-tailed bats.

Visitors, who gather in bleacher seats set atop the tunnel, arrive before sunset to watch them take flight. The colony, which is made up of about three million migratory, nesting bats, is active from May through October. The bats begin to leave for Mexico at the sign of the first cold front. They usually don't emerge on nights of heavy rain.

If you arrive early, you can hike the half-mile-long Old Tunnel Nature Trail to the tunnel entrance. It's fairly steep. The tunnel was dug in the early part of the 20th century to provide passage through a 2,300-feet-high ridge on Mount Alamo.

HANGING WITH THE BATS

WHAT: Old Tunnel State Park (800) 792-1112, or (866) 978-2287 for emergence times.

WHERE: 10619 Old San Antonio Rd., Fredericksburg, TX. Located 11 miles south of Fredericksburg.

COST: Free for upper level viewing, but a $5 activity fee is charged for the lower level.

PRO TIP: Old San Antonio Road, off US 290, is a winding, scenic drive through the rural Hill Country that leads past many historic stone homesteads and tiny settlements enroute to the tunnel. You'll find great burgers and a pleasant outdoor bar at Alamo Springs Café, adjacent to the state park.

Top: *The tunnel provided a short cut through the rugged hills between Fredericksburg and San Antonio.*

Bottom left: *A railroad tunnel unused since the 1940s holds one of the largest bat colonies in the Hill Country.*

Bottom right: *Flights of steps and a steep trail lead down to the tunnel.*

It was used for more than four decades to carry goods between Fredericksburg and San Antonio. The Texas Parks and Wildlife Department took over the property in 1991 and it opened to the public as Old Tunnel State Park.

When the railroad left town, not many could see the light at the end of the tunnel, but the tiny creatures who live there now like the dark, just fine.

GUEST WHO?

Did Lincoln lodge at the Schmitz Hotel, or was it just a prank?

Have you ever looked at the old registers of quaint hotels? If you have, you might find that familiar names have preceded you. The Schmitz Hotel, now known as the Schmitz Bed and Breakfast, in downtown New Braunfels is just such a place.

An important link to the German immigrants and their role as town founders, the building was purchased by the New Braunfels Conservation Society in 1969. The hotel's facade had been altered but the Society restored it, operating it as a bed and breakfast. It is now privately owned and operates as a short-term vacation rental.

The Schmitz Hotel, named for its owner Jacob Schmitz, a German immigrant and a founding father of New Braunfels, was built in 1851. Stagecoaches brought travelers seeking a night's rest on the trip from San Antonio to Austin.

First called the Plaza hotel because of its location near the New Braunfels plaza, the limestone and cedar two-story business intrigued Schmitz, who was already a successful owner of a stagecoach post on Seguin Street.

He bought the Plaza from its owner in 1857. After adding a third floor with a balcony in 1873, he gave the hotel his own name. The coming of the railroad brought more business to this thriving hotel, which brought in visitors until its closing in 1910.

COME TO THE PLAZA

WHAT: The Schmitz Bed and Breakfast (Formerly Schmitz Hotel)

WHERE: 471 Main Plaza, New Braunfels, TX

COST: The five apartments rent for a two-night minimum with prices ranging from $125 to $395, depending on the season. Reservations at historicschmitz.com or call (830) 660-7738.

PRO TIP: Put on your comfortable walking shoes to see the nearby attractions of New Braunfels, shops and restaurants, Schlitterbahn Waterpark, and the Comal River.

Right: *The Schmitz hotel, the oldest lodging place in Fredericksburg, still welcomes guests.*

Inset: *The hotel has hosted many famous people since it opened in 1851.*

Fortunately hotel registers were rescued from being burned with the trash in a 1910 fire, giving us evidence of illustrious visitors and their opinions of their stay. Those famous visitors included Frederick Law Olmsted, the architect of New York's Central Park. In his hotel review in 1854, he noted the attention to detail in the rooms, the caliber of service, and the excellent meals which he noted did not contain pork and were not fried. Sidney Lanier, noted Southern poet, visited in 1872 and praised the gentlemanly treatment of female travelers. Politicians and government officials stayed here, including Texas hero Sam Houston.

However, one purported visitor stands above all others. His actual presence at the hotel and the authenticity of his registry signature remain a good story but unverifiable. A tall bearded fellow from Illinois was said to have passed through the town and stayed at the inn. The name Abraham Lincoln in the register has added another layer to the storied history of Jacob Schmitz's hotel, in spite of the belief that his inclusion was a prank.

Visit the Freiheit School House building on the Plaza at 1300 Churchill Drive for exhibits detailing the Schmitz history as well as photos of its transformation over the past 150 years.

SUNSETS AT THE STONEWALL

What quaint motel invites you to toast the past?

You can still step back in time and enjoy the charms of an authentic motor lodge in the Hill Country. The L-shaped Stonewall Motor Lodge was built in 1964 and became a home base for the Secret Service as well as the National Press when the area's most famous citizen came to town. President Lyndon B. Johnson's ranch, often dubbed the Texas White House, is a neighbor.

The original owners who built the motel to deal with the multitude of new visitors were Tillie and Kermitt Hahne. After the swearing in of President Johnson as 37th president in 1963, the world would get to know of the beauty and hospitality of the Hill Country. Close friends of Lyndon and Lady Bird, they put out the red carpet for a multitude of politicians and celebrities, introducing them to the delight that is Texas barbecue. Tillie cranked gallons of peach ice cream, using fruit from their orchards.

The motel's 12 rooms saw a diverse group of visitors. One was Walter Cronkite of CBS News who conducted multiple interviews at the ranch. On a Sunday morning, you would see reporters eating a quick breakfast in their cars, waiting for the presidential motorcade to take LBJ to church. The motor lodge had a Press Room with a darkroom for photographers.

Purchased by Anita and Lance Lubke and five other couples in 2018, the iconic motel underwent a renovation

Once headquarters for the White House Press Corps, the Stonewall Motor Lodge shines again.

Top: *The rooftop deck at the refurbished Stonewall Motor Lodge provides a place to toast a Hill Country sunset in the heart of the wine country.*

Top right inset: *The lodge, which is close to the LBJ Ranch, is renovated as a more comfortable version of a 1960s motel.*

Bottom left inset: *After Johnson became president, press coverage popularized the Hill Country as a tourist destination.*

Bottom right inset: *The Press Room, outfitted for reporters who covered the president, features photographs of President Johnson.*

that restored the rustic charm. You still drive up to your room with its turquoise door and welcoming window, but now you can enjoy new amenities such as an observation deck to enjoy a Texas sunset and a glass of wine. An open air event barn at the rear of the property hosts local musicians. The most popular of the original 12 rooms? It's the one dubbed The Press Room. Inside you'll discover photos of the folks who brought prominence to the small town, including charming ones of LBJ with his grandchildren and his beloved dogs.

A PIECE OF THE PAST

WHAT: Stonewall Motor Lodge

WHERE: 14818 E US 290, Stonewall, TX

COST: $175 for cabins; $129 for rooms

PRO TIP: Ask for the availability of room #8, the Press Room.

AVOID THE REDHEAD

How did bowling get itself out of the gutter?

Bowling came to our shores in the 1700s. The early game had a European flavor with its nine pins in a diamond formation. The game was a mainstay in 19th century American taverns and saloons, a far cry from the wholesome family bowling lanes that sprang up across 20th century America. The early games gained an unsavory reputation, believed by citizens to be encouragers of laziness, drunkenness, gambling, and crime. In the 1830s the games were banned in many cities.

How did Texas handle this? Why ban totally when you can tax? The 1st Congress of the Republic of Texas in 1837 levied a $150 per year tax on nine-pin bowling. Today all bowling in our state operates with this tax. The game flourished in bowling clubs which encourage family play. In the Hill Country the large number of German immigrants flocked to these clubs for wholesome fun, food, and social activities.

Nine-pin bowling declined in popularity with the advent of 10-pin bowling with its automated setup, multiple lanes, and electronic scoring. However, it is still alive and well in the Hill Country. The setup and scoring are quite different. Men and women, teens, and octogenarians share the load of knocking down pins. The pin setup is a diamond shape with the ninth pin occupying its center. That pin is often called the redhead. The goal is to knock down the other eight and leave that center pin standing. Scoring is different as well, involving an evening of

---

This is a piece of the social framework immigrants brought from Europe. It's a sport that has a decreased American footprint, but families have kept the lanes active in the Hill Country.

Left: *Favored by German settlers, nine-pin bowling became popular in Blanco and many other Hill Country towns.*

Left inset: *The object of nine-pin bowling is to avoid the red pin in the center.*

Center inset: *Freiheit operates a local nine-pin establishment.*

Right inset: *Solms Bowling Club is one of the oldest.*

pitting your team of six players against another team on the way to achieving the highest score.

One way these clubs have kept their members is with a low annual fee and the welcoming of family members as pinsetters. These small venues do not have automated pinsetters or electronic scoring. You pay your dues with fees and labor as well. Some of the best players today started out as pinsetters for their family's team. It's a job that requires concentration and dexterity with untangling pins.

Venues that still have nine-pin bowling are Blanco's six lane Bowling Club, which is being restored, and New Braunfels's the Barbarossa, the Solms, and the Freiheit. These clubs are private organizations, but some will allow non members to participate if there is space.

SKILL COUNTS

WHAT: Nine-pin bowling

WHERE: Hill Country nine-pin clubs, most are private

WHEN: Hours are fluid

COST: Fees set by clubs if space for non members is available.

PRO TIP: Blanco's Bowling Club, now being restored with a café, is one of the easiest clubs to visit, located on the town square in Blanco.

STOLLEN GOODS?

How many ways can you say delicious in Alsatian?

Enter Haby's Alsatian Bakery in Castroville and you'll find yourself in another country. Be prepared to master some new words for delicious pastries. Stollen, kugelhopf, and tasty macaroons fill the glass cases, tempting customers. Founded by Stanley Haby in 1974, the baked goods are a blend of the pastries of France, Germany, and Switzerland. All of this fruit-filled goodness comes together in the French region responsible for this style, Alsace. The man who brought this culture to the Hill Country was Henri Castro, who led his fellow Alsatians to this region in 1844.

Castroville itself has kept the flavor of the Alsace region not only in food but in architecture. Look for the signature elements of sloped roofs, decorative timbers, window boxes, and shutters. You'll feel that you've been transported to a European village. There are, in fact, folks of Alsatian descent here who still speak the language.

When you visit, you have a choice of many sweet treats, and the employees are quite friendly and patient with those customers who just can't decide. Sugar cookies are a hit, and you can expect beautifully decorated ones often tied to a seasonal theme. The macaroons are a signature item. You get to choose between the coconut filled cookie version and the Turkish variety featuring pecans and dates. The kugelhopf is large and has the consistency of a sweet cake. Add a little butter

COMFORT FOOD SPOKEN HERE

WHAT: Haby's Alsatian Bakery

WHERE: 207 US 90 E, Castroville, TX

WHEN: Monday through Saturday, 5:30 a.m. to 7 p.m.; Closed on Sundays.

COST: Two pastries and a cup of coffee costs $3

PRO TIP: Ask for a sample if you're unsure as to what to choose. They are used to it.

Top left: *Tasty pastries welcome customers.*

Top inset: *The bakery features everything from bread to bridal cakes along with many Alsatian specialties.*

Bottom inset: *A mural of early Castroville decorates Haby's Alsatian bakery.*

and jelly and enjoy one along with a hot cup of coffee. The popular stollen is a bun-size pastry full of cherries or blueberries. Frequent customers request donuts, fruit pies, and fritters. Haby's caters to the locals with creative and artistic birthday cakes made-to-order and wedding cakes good enough to have received a thumbs-up from *The Knot*, the go-to publication for all things bridal. Because it's a bakery, you can purchase bread. However, you are offered many choices: pumpkin, Hearth bread, rye, pumpernickel, as well as wheat. The smell is heavenly.

The bakers at Haby's come to work every day before the sun rises. It's a labor of love, getting ready for hungry customers.

MAGICAL MEDINA

Where can you tube a river and leave the crowds behind?

Kayaking and tubing are two of the most popular river pastimes in Texas. With all the fresh water in the state, there are an infinite number of places to enjoy it. However, many are crowded with folks seeking relief from the summer heat. The hotter the weather, the more you can expect traffic jams on the rivers. It can be hard to find a space to squeeze into.

If you want a pastoral river experience, try the Medina River. Flowing for 120 miles, it is renowned for its cool, clear, calm waters. Only 30 to 40 feet wide, it offers floaters a good look at its limestone outcroppings on its shore as well as its abundant plant life. You can float down this waterway in a tube, enjoying open spaces and beautiful scenery. One of the greatest benefits is the canopy of trees that shades the river and gives protection to tubers. Look for cypress, live oak, and maples. This diversity of arboreal beauty makes for a fabulous fall as well. Red autumn leaves dance in the swirls and eddies of the Medina.

A great place to enjoy river fun is at Bandera, Texas. This town in the Hill Country is famously called the "Cowboy Capital of the World." Known for its role in the great Texas cattle drives,

MEANDERING DOWN THE MEDINA

WHAT: The Medina River experience

WHERE: Bandera, TX, less than an hour from San Antonio

COST: Rental of tubes and kayaks at Medina River Company, shuttle to river included: tube $20; kayak $50.

PRO TIP: Glass containers and styrofoam are prohibited, but you can bring beverages.

Top left: *The Medina River meanders through a tunnel of towering cypress trees.*
Photo courtesy of Wikimedia

Top right: *The spring-fed river is often less crowded than the Guadalupe and other popular Hill Country streams.*
Photo courtesy of Stewart Tomlinson, US Geological Survey

Bottom: *The Medina River shuttle provides tubes, kayaks, and transportation to the river from Bandera.*

the rustic town wears its mantle proudly, holding rodeos during the summer and welcoming visitors to its dude ranches. However, the fresh water is a huge draw for visitors here. Kayaking is popular, too, because of the calm water. You can bring your own kayaks or tubes or try the Medina River Company in Bandera for rentals of both.

Walk along the river and enjoy the views of the clear water. You'll see a variety of aquatic life darting over the smooth rocks that line the river bed.

DIAMONDS IN THE STREAM

What Texas fish glitters like the gem it truly is?

Lupe, the Guadalupe bass, glistens on the sunlit perch it enjoys in the Louise Hays Park Fountain Plaza in Kerrville. Adjacent to the Guadalupe River, this park provides a perfect aquatic home. Installed in 2017, this colorful symbol of Texas appears to leap from the azure waters at its base. Its mouth is open; its body is arched, ready for a fight as though to tease nearby fishermen. Gigi Miller, the sculptor, grew up in the Kerrville area and hooked her first fish while at summer camp. It is one of her fondest childhood memories.

Her sculpture of the bass is an example of ferrocement (fashioning a cement coat over mesh or rebar). *Lupe* wears a coat of many colored mosaic ceramic tiles which are dear to the residents of Kerrville. The summer before installation, a craft camp was held to give people the opportunity to contribute to the artwork. Tiles were created at that craft fair.

Imagine yourself bathing your feet on the bank of the Guadalupe River on a hot summer day. Train your eyes on the currents of the magnificent spring-fed waters. What are you looking for? The darting motion of a most popular fish, the Guadalupe bass. Its small green body ranges from lime to olive shading, dotted with diamond shapes. It enjoys a buffet of local insects and likes to seek a good hiding place in the rocky river bed. Unlike its bigger relatives, the largest one caught was 3 lb. 11 oz. in 1983 in Lake Travis.

So why would such an average creature be named state fish? It is not well known outside of the state because it lives only in the clear waters of the streams and rivers of the Hill Country. Texas is famous for its "bigger is better" philosophy of life. However, this little fellow has something quite important

Gigi Miller's sculpture Lupe *glistens in a park beside the Guadalupe River in Kerrville.*

SWIMMING WITH THE FISHES

WHAT: *Lupe*, ceramic sculpture

WHERE: Louise Hays Park, 202 Thompson Dr., Kerrville, TX

WHEN: 10 a.m. to 11 p.m.

COST: Free

PRO TIP: Visit the Guadalupe River to look for Lupe's relatives.

going for it. It is a fighter, prized by fly fisherman. Hook him and he will take your line on quite a ride over, under, and around river rocks, as he zigs and zags expertly in the clear streams.

Lupe represents one of the most important aspects of the geography of the area. Small but mighty it brings attention to the importance of the state's abundance of fresh water streams and the species that live in them.

This fish is a rare species listed as near threatened. Fishermen often do catch and release to help preserve its numbers.

CURTAIN UP

Where can you see a classic horse opera and listen to live music in an authentic 1930s movie house?

Drive through any small Texas town and you're likely to find a shuttered movie theater with its dusty coming attractions' display speaking of better days. However, some places in the Hill Country have decided to turn back the hands of time.

This desire to bring back that which has been lost is a part of Bertram's tip of the hat to its early citizens. The original town fathers saw a need for a respite from the hard times of the Great Depression and commissioned the Bertram Amusement Company to build a theater in 1935. The new addition to the small town of less than 700 residents enjoyed sold out performances. Their hopes for the new business were quite high as seen in the local paper, the *Bertram Enterprise*, in 1935: "This modern theater will be one of the prettiest theaters to be found in Texas in a town the size of Bertram, or even larger."

In downtown Bertram, the movie house is back in business. In 2009, Zach Hamilton and Lance Regier convinced the owner to sell them the theater which had sat unused since the 1980s.

The renovation was a big undertaking that involved following leads as to original elements missing from this building. Where was the marquee that once flanked the building front? In a dairy barn! Want some popcorn? You'll get a bag popped in the original machine. The period display windows greet you with notices of classic movies and upcoming band performances. Everything inside reminds you of the Art Deco interiors so popular in the 1930s. Authentic sconces, which

The Globe and its owners have heeded the original call for an iconic experience.

Left: *The refurbished Globe Theater in Bertram hosts live music and movies.*

Right: *It opened in 1935.*

Inset: *It was designed to be a rich experience for moviegoers.*

bathe the seating area with a soft glow, flank the walls. The huge curtain parts to reveal a Globe Theater mural behind the stage. The seating which includes a comfortable mezzanine has been refurbished with 244 plush burgundy period chairs.

Now the Globe is home to classic western movies, live country western music, birthday parties, weddings, and an occasional car show with vintage vehicles lining the street. For a concert, you'll want to wear your most comfortable boots because the downstairs will be rocking and rolling with folks dancing to live performances in front of the stage.

ENTERTAINMENT TONIGHT

WHAT: The Globe Theater

WHERE: 132 W Vaughan St., Bertram, TX

COST: Check the website for events and ticket prices. Purchase tickets online or at the door. The theater itself has a cash only policy.

PRO TIP: Check out the attention to detail in this restoration project, extending to the door handles and period turquoise and cream tiles that cover the lobby floor.

FOOD OF THE GODS

What drink can be found in the Bible as well as in the works of Chaucer and Shakespeare?

The oldest alcoholic drink in the world has found its way to the Hill Country. Mead is a beverage fermented from honey, yeast, and water. The more honey in the mix, the sweeter the drink. For a unique brew, you can add your favorite fruit or vegetable to the mix. It's up to you. According to aficionados, drink it as you would wine or beer.

This drink has enjoyed increasing popularity in the past decade with new meaderies opening nationwide. Why the increase? Possibly the main ingredient, honey. It has a reputation for being a healthy food, bearing probiotics. Or it could be that a drink of ages past has found its way back into the national consciousness. If you've gone to a Renaissance Fair, you've been offered a glass of mead.

For those who want to try mead, come to Texas Mead Works which is a part of the Blue Lotus Winery in Hye, Texas. Off US 290, the winery and mead works are part of the Fredericksburg Wine Road, a long line of vineyards and wineries presenting the products of Texas-grown grapes. Indeed the Blue Lotus winery uses Texas grapes grown in West Texas and Seguin, the home base of the winery. The building for tasting is quite appropriate in that it is barrel-shaped and has a beautiful wooden interior.

The owners of Blue Lotus Winery and Texas Mead Works, Melissa and Michael Poole, opened their Hye location in 2018, serving a variety of wines, white and red as well as their various meads. Michael got his start in brewing in Washington State in the early 90s. Having much experience with wine and beer, he happened upon a meadery and added that to his wish list for his future business.

Come for a tasting of wine and mead from 11 a.m. to 6 p.m. Thursday to Sunday. For $15 you get five pours of wine, mead, or a combination. Bottled wine and mead are for sale. The Blueberry

Top inset: *The winery uses many local fruits to create new varieties of mead.*

Bottom: *The Blue Lotus Winery and Texas Mead Works uses old methods to create modern day mead.*

Bottom inset: *The winery can be found on the 290 Wine Trail.*

MEAD 101

WHAT: Blue Lotus Winery and Texas Mead Works

WHERE: 8500 W US 290, Hye, TX

COST: $15 for a five-pour tasting

PRO TIP: Be adventurous and try an assortment of wine and mead.

Jasmine mead is very popular and can be purchased for $20. If you like a little kick with your honeyed drink, try a bottle of Jalapeño mead for $20, my personal favorite. They also serve St. Michael's Mead, an alternative to beer which is a gluten free carbonated version. Michael Poole, head winemaker, will guide you in your search.

The term honeymoon has its roots in Old English. The European custom of giving newlyweds enough mead to last a full month was to ensure a happy beginning to the marriage.

157

HEADING FOR A HUNDRED

Where can you watch a rodeo and dance under the stars?

Crider's Rodeo and Dancehall has stood the test of Texas time and stayed in the saddle. Started by Walter and Audrey Crider in 1925 as a rodeo fundraiser for the local school, the July 4th event caught on. The popularity of the rodeo brought a call for a dance floor and some good music.

Imagine a warm summer evening. You smell the tangy barbecue smoking and the juicy hamburgers grilling. Grab a bite and a brew; then sit down at one of the picnic tables by the dance floor. You will probably meet someone from the area who is a regular. It's a great way to learn about life in a small town in the Hill Country. The sounds of the Mark Odom Band float on the breeze from the dance floor near the river. Dancers on the floor run the gamut from five-year-olds dancing on their dad's boots to octogenarians showing the younger crowd how it's done. You never know who might be there doing the two-step

SADDLE UP AND DANCE

WHAT: Crider's Rodeo and Dancehall

WHERE: 2310 TX-39, Hunt, TX

WHEN: The season begins on Memorial Day weekend and ends on Labor Day weekend. Rodeo starts Saturday night at 8 p.m.; Music at the dance hall from 9 p.m. to 1 a.m. Saturdays.

COST: $15 for 13+, seniors $5, under 13 is free

PRO TIP: Catfish dinners are Friday nights at 6 p.m. during the summer.

The rodeo and dance at Crider's has been going on since 1925.

Top: *Outdoor dances under the stars start after the rodeo.*

Bottom left: *The night begins with the introduction of the flag and the singing of the national anthem.*

Bottom right: *Some of the participants are a little more stubborn than others.*

next to you. On a typical Saturday night, the crowd might include schoolteachers, professional athletes, actors, truck drivers, and maybe even an astronaut.

The rodeo is winding down in the adjacent arena. It's some of the best fun Hunt, Texas, has to offer. An open rodeo, participants aren't professionals. Brave bull riders battle the clock to see how long they can stay on board, kicking up a pile of dust while doing it. Mutton busting brings in the young crowd of future rodeo stars. To qualify for riding a wooly creature, you have to weigh in at under 50 pounds. It's a popular event for the short crowd.

Crider's doesn't just cater to the Saturday night crowd. It's also a wedding venue with a beautiful place for the event on the edge of the Guadalupe. Where else can you calf rope a steer or tie a wedding knot?

MUSIC AND A MEAL

Where can you go when you need a great burger and fries and some live music?

Freiheit is the German word for freedom and that is the name the early German settlers gave the small farming community.

HISTORY WITH A SIDE OF FRIES

WHAT: Freiheit Country Store

WHERE: 2157 FM 1101, New Braunfels, TX

WHEN: Weekdays 11 a.m.–10 p.m.; Thursday through Saturday 11:00 a.m.–11 p.m.; closed Monday

COST: Burgers are $6 to $12

PRO TIP: Save room for a slice of pie.

Well, now you are free to order a burger your way, sip a tasty, cold brew, and stay for the live music at night. The Freiheit Country Store about three miles northeast of New Braunfels has been serving folks since 1889. It's housed in a rustic wooden and metal building with an interior that is perfect for its use. Corrugated tin ceilings, red brick pillars, and German signs speak of the casual but friendly vibe of the place. You might hear someone next to you say, "Prosit," when lifting a beer glass with a friend. Drinking to one's health is very much a part of the German community. One of the store's t-shirts proclaims, "It's a burger joint with a German heritage."

Mike Reimer purchased this place in 2006 and added to it over the years, installing a stage outdoors for bands as well as a patio. A native of New Braunfels, he liked the humble little store that hadn't changed in all the years it served the community.

The menu is definitely geared to beef lovers. Hamburgers run the gamut from "Sloppy" to "Extreme" to "Oinker," which boasts bacon on the cheeseburger. If you're a Reimer family member, you'll have a burger named for you: the Cody, the Kerry, and the Big Mike Double, in memory of the owner who died in 2020.

Top left: *The Freiheit Country Store has been serving customers since 1889.*

Top right: *Rustic decorations and vintage memorabilia greet patrons.*

Bottom left: *Visitors can enjoy live music under the stars behind the store.*

Bottom right: *They don't offer a shave and a haircut, but they do serve beef.*

The music nights often charge no cover, and the outdoor area is heated. You can enjoy a starry Texas night, good food, and boot-tapping live music.

The Freiheit keeps the German heritage alive with good food and cold brews in this small community.

CELEBRATED CUKES

Where can you buy a nostalgic antique sign along with a side of pickles?

Fickle Pickles was the brain child of "the pickle lady" Billie A. Shaw. A lover of antiques and gardening, she put her dual passions to work in her little store in Boerne, Texas. The small, rustic vine-covered cottage holds a secret, the recipe for what many fans of Fickle Pickles call the best example of a brined cucumber in the world. The thin-sliced pickle with its signature wavy surface has been bringing in customers to Boerne for decades and finding fans in far flung places such as Finland and Japan. They do ship abroad. These pickles have gone home with a few celebrities as well. Former Governor George W. Bush visited and bought a few bottles and 007 Pierce Brosnan likes them, too.

Shaw used a recipe that had been in her family for decades, pickling for family and friends. Cucumbers from her bountiful garden eventually found their way into jars at home. Quarts turned into gallons of pickles. But you can't keep a perfect pickle under wraps and its fame spread, moving Shaw to open a pickle/antique business in 1987. Her marketing strategy was simple. Give the public a free taste of the crinkle-cut slices and sell them a few jars. Today the business model is the same. Let the pickle speak for itself.

Dating back to Biblical times, the pickle inspires aficionados to find the best ways to use it. Whether it be Deviled eggs; tuna, egg, and chicken salad; or the topping for a juicy burger, these

SAMPLE A SUMPTUOUS SLICE

WHAT: Fickle Pickles

WHERE: 118 S Main St., Boerne, TX

WHEN: Monday through Saturday 10 a.m. to 5 p.m., Sunday noon to 4 p.m.

COST: $12 to $22

PRO TIP: Don't throw out the pickle juice. You can use it for marinade for all types of meat or to baste your barbecue.

Left: *The samples disappear quickly.*

Right: *Fickle Pickles is one of the most popular shops in downtown Boerne.*

Inset: *You can purchase spicy or regular.*

tart goodies will make you pucker up. The folks who work at the shop are Texas friendly and will give you their tried and true recipes. Fickle Pickles are both sweet and savory as well as deliciously crunchy. The company produces only two types of the signature product: regular and "red 'X' marks the spot" spicy. You'll find both sides of the pickle aisle make arguments in support of their favorite. However, the regular outsells the spicy, but it can not be called bland according to the owners.

Mrs. Shaw's daughter Lisa Obriotti took over the day to day business in the early 2000s. After Mrs. Shaw's death in 2008, Obriotti started to answer to the title "Pickle Lady's daughter." She expanded the business over the years, moving out of the Shaw's kitchen to a commercial kitchen as well as opening locations in Gruene, Bandera, and New Braunfels. She's mighty proud to keep her mother's legacy alive.

Fickle Pickles were once featured on the *Martha Stewart Show*, enlightening the lifestyle guru about the sweet and spicy Texas snack.

163

MASSACRE OF A WAGON TRAIN

How did a journey into the Hill Country turn out so tragically for the Webster Wagon Train?

Always covetous of new territory, Mirabeau B. Lamar, president of the Texas Republic, wanted to push the frontier west. The saga of a lost wagon train that ventured into the Hill Country in 1839 proved what a dangerous place it could be. The Webster family wagon train started out with grand dreams. It ended in an almost forgotten grave in a tiny cemetery in the Austin suburb of Leander.

John Webster, who came to Texas from Virginia, couldn't wait to move west. In the summer of 1839, he filled wagons with supplies and recruited 11 hardy men to guard him, his wife, Dolly, and their son, Booker, 11, and four-year-old daughter, Martha. They were going to claim a league of land in Burnet County. They made is as far as a hill rise on the North San Gabriel River. That's where they saw a war party of as many as 300 Comanches. Turning back, they reached Brushy Creek near the present town of Leander before the Comanches overtook them. The settlers formed the wagons in a circle and fought most of the day. All were killed, except for Dolly and her

DANGEROUS JOURNEY

WHAT: Webster Massacre

WHERE: A Texas historical marker is at the Davis Cemetery where the victims are buried together. It is located on Ranch Road 2243, about 1 ½ miles east of the US 183 toll road.

COST: Free

PRO TIP: Later in life, Martha married and returned to the original land grant to found the town of Strickland in 1853. It prospered for a few years, but became a ghost town when the railroad bypassed it. She left a first-hand account of the courageous struggle her mother suffered to make her escape.

Victims of the Webster Wagon Train Massacre rest in an almost forgotten grave in a tiny cemetery in Leander.

children, who were taken prisoner. According to some accounts, Dolly attempted to escape six times with her daughter until the two finally made it to safety in San Antonio in 1840. Booker was ransomed the following year.

It's said that noted frontiersman Edward Burleson led a rescue party that found the remains of the victims. Their bones were gathered in a wagon box and buried in a common grave at what is now the Davis Cemetery, located near the site of the massacre at Brushy Creek.

The fate of one group of travelers proved how dangerous the Hill Country once was.

A ROAD RUNS THROUGH IT

Where can you take a drive through some of the most scenic beauty of the Hill Country?

If you travel a winding road near Hunt known as Texas 39, you will be in cowboy country, full of scenic views, horse pastures, bustling rodeo arenas, and clear waters.

RIDING BY A RIVER

WHAT: Texas 39

WHERE: Start outside of Kerrville at Ingram and continue to Hunt

COST: Free

PRO TIP: There are picnic tables at several river crossings that provide a place to enjoy the view.

This area has a history of ranching with an abundance of cattle, sheep, and goats. The Guadalupe River which runs by the highway provided early settlers with sustenance. Now it is a passage to summer fun and recreation.

Between Ingram and Hunt, you'll see the popular swimming hole Schumacher's Crossing with its clear water and picturesque rapids framed by cypress trees. If the water level is cooperating, stop for a rest and take a swim.

Generations of youngsters have traveled this road to experience one of the summer camps that line the river. Dedicated to learning to appreciate life through nature, these area camps have riding arenas and horses available for campers. Heart O' the Hills camp brings back childhood memories with its smell of fresh grass and sounds of noisy evening crickets. Since 1953 the camp has beckoned to children. The grounds are on both sides of the Guadalupe River, providing abundant water activities. Camp la Junta for boys is literally "a gathering place." Campers come here for skeet shooting, mountain biking, and horseback riding. Teddy Roosevelt would've appreciated this

Left: *Texas 39 runs beside the Guadalupe River.*

Right: *Waldemar and other famous youth camps steeped in tradition make their homes nestled along the river.*

camp, for a prestigious group of campers called "The Rough Riders" takes on a camping and ranching exercise, taking care of livestock, as well as cooking and sleeping under the stars.

Camp Mystic, founded in 1926, is a short jog on Farm Road 1340 at Hunt. It is a girl's camp dedicated to fostering independence, bringing in generations of loyal campers. Look for the sign proclaiming Mystic which sits on top of a hill called Sky High. Girls on teams participate in sports and activities daily which bring about a sense of camaraderie. Years later campers still greet one another as teammates. Camp Waldemar, another girl's camp started in 1926, sits on the Guadalupe River nearby and stresses outdoor activities as well as creative arts. The mission is to help young girls gain independence. If you've ever been a Waldemar camper, you've joined one of the Texas tribes that form a sense of belonging and cooperation in their members.

Keep a lookout for high game fencing, for you might see exotic animals resting under trees. If you're thirsty or hungry, try the Hunt Store for a soft drink and a brisket sandwich or a juicy burger. A favorite of locals, the Store is a place to pass the time or discuss the news and weather while enjoying a cup of coffee.

The clear waters of the Guadalupe and its beautiful topography offer many opportunities for travelers to cool off and enjoy nature on a hot Texas day.

A BISON FOUND
AND A WATERFALL LOST

Whatever happened to the falls in Marble Falls?

The "great marble falls on the Colorado" that gave Marble Falls its name is at the bottom of Lake Marble Falls now. Bison that once roamed these hills are long gone too. You can find out what happened to both of them at a fine small-town museum that's almost a secret missed by most travelers passing through.

A few blocks northwest of the downtown business district, the Falls on the Colorado Museum is housed in a stout, two-story granite building that was one of the most substantial structures in the area when it was finished in 1891. It was once part of a university started by town founder Adam Rankin Johnson and later served as a public school for decades. Now it houses almost 6,000-square-feet of exhibits.

An extensive display of historical photographs includes many that show the falls when it was a well-known landmark, popular for swimming and picnic outings. The water source, with its potential to power future industries, is what drew Johnson, to found the town. He was a Civil War general, known as "Stovepipe" Johnson, because he once used a fake cannon made of wagon wheels and a stovepipe to capture a Union arsenal. Near the end of the war, Johnson was blinded accidentally by a shot fired by his own forces. In spite of losing his sight, Johnson went on to amazing accomplishments that included leading cattle drives and founding a town.

Some of the museum's exhibits reach back to prehistoric times. One of the most recent attractions, which went on view

At the Falls on the Colorado Museum, a town's colorful history isn't just water under the bridge.

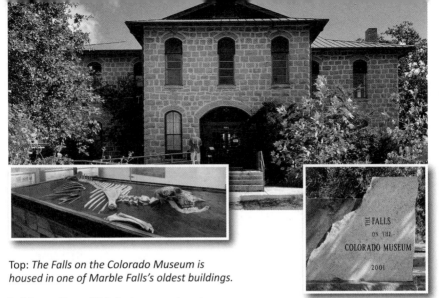

Top: *The Falls on the Colorado Museum is housed in one of Marble Falls's oldest buildings.*

Left inset: *One exhibit features an almost complete skeleton of a 700-year-old bison found in the area.*

Right inset: *The museum's exhibits help explain what happened to the falls at Marble Falls.*

in 2018, is the almost complete skeleton of a 700-year-old bison. The animal, which was estimated to weigh at least 1,200 pounds when it roamed the Texas hills, is displayed the way it looked when it was excavated. Ryan Murray found it on a bank along Rocky Creek on his father's ranch near Briggs. The female was named Rockie after the creek she was found on. Rockie is viewed by hundreds of school children each year at Marble Falls Elementary School, which neighbors the museum. No matter what age you are, it's a good place to learn a lot about the colorful history of Marble Falls.

LOST AND FOUND

WHAT: Falls on the Colorado Museum

WHERE: 2001 Broadway, Marble Falls, TX

COST: Free, donations are welcome. The museum opens 10 a.m. to 2 p.m. Tuesday through Saturday; fallsmueum.org, or (830) 798-2157.

PRO TIP: The museum is made from some of the same "sunset red" granite quarried from Granite Mountain in Marble Falls to build the Texas capitol and other landmarks around the world. Early explorers thought the falls were made of granite too, but the water tumbled over limestone so polished by the current it resembled granite.

BUILT TO LAST

English-born architect Alfred Giles built elegant buildings that dot the Hill Country, but was his biggest dream way too big for Texas?

Ranching was good. Reconstruction was over. Texans were feeling prosperous toward the end of the 1800s. Alfred Giles built the stuff dreams are made of. Educated in England, he came to America at the age of 20, after a bout of rheumatic fever. He hoped the fresh air would help him recover. Giles settled in San Antonio. He designed dozens of homes and buildings and soon his artistry was in demand across the Hill Country.

Landmarks of his design remain in almost every Hill Country town. His projects included at least 11 courthouses across Texas. Fredericksburg has one of the finest surviving examples of his work. Built of native limestone in the Romanesque Revival style, the courthouse is preserved as the Pioneer Memorial Library. In Fredericksburg, Giles also designed the Bank of Fredericksburg at 120 E Main Street (now a real estate office) and the Morris Ranch School House, now privately owned.

In Kerrville, he designed the Schreiner Mansion, Schreiner Bank, and Schreiner Store. In Bandera, Giles built the Old Bandera County Jail. His buildings fill the Main Street historic district in Comfort, where Giles established the 13,000-acre Hillingdon Ranch, named for his birthplace in England. When he traveled to

LANDMARK MAKER

WHAT: Alfred Giles, architect of Hill Country courthouses and many other buildings

WHERE: Pioneer Memorial Library, 115 W Main St., Fredericksburg, TX. Originally the Gillespie County Courthouse, built in 1882.

COST: Free

PRO TIP: Main Street in Comfort preserves one of the largest clusters of Giles's designs, including the modest Comfort Post Office, built in 1908. His classical designs gave growing towns lasting treasures.

Top left and right: *Giles designed the Romanesque revival courthouse in Fredericksburg, preserved as the Pioneer Memorial Library.*

Bottom left: *Alfred Giles was born in England and designed some of the most elegant courthouses in the Hill Country. Photo courtesy of Institute of Texan Cultures*

Bottom right: *Alfred Giles designed the post office and many other landmarks in Comfort.*

the ranch, Giles brought carrier pigeons along to send messages to his wife in San Antonio. The frontier still had rough edges. Once the stagecoach he was riding to Fredericksburg was stopped by robbers. The experience didn't daunt his love for Texas. Giles revered Texas heroes, especially the martyrs who died at the Alamo. In 1887, he proposed a 118-feet tall monument with an observation deck topped with a sculpture of Davy Crockett. A cenotaph commissioned from local sculptor Pompeo Coppini was selected instead. Giles wasn't discouraged. In 1912, he proposed an 802-feet-tall tower. It would be topped with an observation deck, and telescopes to take in a 100-mile view across the Hill Country by day and illuminated at night by "the most powerful searchlight engineers could devise." A statewide funding effort was started to raise the $2 million to build it, but the effort faded away at the onset of World War I. Giles died in 1920. No Texan ever dreamed bigger.

Alfred Giles built many Hill Country landmarks, but his biggest dream was an 80-story tower at the Alamo that never got off the drawing board.

HIGH ON PIE!

Why is happy hour at the Blue Bonnet Cafe short and sweet?

Happy hours in other places entice diners with offers of spirits and savory snacks. But a pie happy hour may just take the cake. When you just have to have that sweet treat on a late afternoon, this should be your destination. The Blue Bonnet Cafe in Marble Falls will set you up with a generous slice of any pie in the house for the price of $5, including drink. Fruit, nut, cream varieties. They are all there. But the unbelievable meringues may be the star of the daily show. Be sure to find your way to the cafe's happy hour from 3 p.m. to 5 p.m. Mondays through Fridays.

These delicious desserts are made daily and are the gem in the crown of the Blue Bonnet. Walk in the door and at the end of a narrow entrance hall, you'll see the kitchen full of the artisans responsible for the 15 versions of these star attractions being made. These are hard-working bakers who know how to make a silky chocolate cream or a "high as an elephant's eye" lemon meringue. Their expert skills keep a huge glass case filled daily.

MARVELOUS MERINGUE

WHAT: Pie Happy Hour

WHERE: Blue Bonnet Cafe, 211 N US 281, Marble Falls, TX

WHEN: 3 p.m.–5 p.m. Monday through Friday

COST: $5 per slice, drink included

PRO TIP: Read the articles about the cafe that line the hallway entrance. They are a testament to the longevity of a place that honors baking artistry.

Contrary to popular belief, the Blue Bonnet Cafe is not named for the state wildflower. It actually refers to a woman's blue hat.

Top: *The Blue Bonnet Café holds a pie happy hour on weekdays.*

Bottom: *Pies rise to the sky.*

The iconic Blue Bonnet Cafe has been serving up Texas-sized comfort food since 1929. Sitting on the edge of US 281, this diner offers everything from chicken fried steak and eggs to sour cream enchiladas. However, the Kemper family who have owned the cafe since 1981 made it the beloved place it is with the mega menu of pies. Belinda Kemper found a way to endear her iconic cafe to locals, tourists, and Hill Country residents. Just fill a huge pie case at the front of the restaurant with an embarrassment of sweet riches. Your biggest problem when it comes to choosing will be whether to take a slice of cream pie or the meringue version. The cream pie is silky rich and decadently creamy while the famous meringue is an airy and light egg white mixture spun until it reaches a gravity defying height. You can get the old dependable such as cherry and pecan, but be adventurous. Peanut butter cream might just satiate your sweet tooth.

If you come here often enough, the friendly waitresses, some of whom have worked here for a quarter of a century, will get to know you and your favorite dishes. It's that kind of atmosphere.

GEMS FOR THE PICKING

If you have sharp eyes, where can you find some carats?

In Dallas or Houston, you have to go to a jewelry store to find a gem. In Mason County, precious stones are just lying on the ground. It's one of the few places where blue topaz, the state gem of Texas, can be found.

Albert McGehee discovered the largest blue topaz ever found in North America in 1904. It's said that he used the 6,480-carat crystal for a doorstop until the Smithsonian Institution bought it for $75 in 1913. The whopper of a gem was on exhibit at the Museum on the Square in Mason until the Smithsonian asked for it back to put on exhibit in 2021. The local museum hopes for its return soon, in the meantime there are quite a few other impressive stones on display.

Or you can go out and find one of your own. Topaz hunters scout for gems for a $20 daily fee

MASON TREASURES

WHAT: Mason County blue topaz

WHERE: Mason Square Museum, northeast side of the square, (325) 347-0507; Mason Country Collectibles, 424 Fort McKavett St., Mason, TX; (325) 347-5249.

COST: Free

PRO TIP: Bring gloves and hiking shoes if you visit the Lindsay Ranch. Finding topaz isn't guaranteed, but quartz, arrow heads, and other interesting finds often turn up. Overnight lodging is available in cabins, starting at $150 per night with a two-night minimum. Day hunts are $20 age 18 and over, $10 age 12–18. Reservations are required; lindsayranch.net, (325) 347-5733.

Rockhounds come to Mason to look for blue topaz, the state gem of Texas. The Smithsonian Institution has the largest one ever found, a 6,480-pound whopper once used a doorstop.

Top: *If you can't find stones on your own, Mason Country Collectibles offers raw and cut stones for sale.*

Inset: *Stones on display include the 587 carat Grand Azure, largest faceted Mason County Topaz known to exist.*

on the Lindsay Ranch. The largest stone ever found there was 263.5 carats. A 20.32 carat beauty turned up in 2017. Most are washed up by rain along Comanche Creek. The best time to look for them is after a heavy downpour when gems are often exposed.

If you don't get lucky, Mason Country Collectibles sells cut stones. Prices start at $100 per carat for clear topaz, and $125 per carat for blue topaz. A cut known as the Texas Star is popular. It's the official gem cut of Texas. The store features a large display of topaz, in its natural state and faceted into cut gems. Some are as large as walnuts. The biggest dazzler is known as The Grand Azure, a 587-carat gem that is the largest faceted Mason County topaz known to exist.

SAY HELLO TO THE TWISTED SISTERS

Are these highways, or are they just paved thrill rides?

Even in the Hill Country, where corkscrew backroads are almost as common as goats, a horseshoe of highways near Vanderpool twists its way to high anxiety above the rest. Their official names are Ranch Roads 337, 336, and 335. But they are known best as the Twisted Sisters.

The roads that rollercoaster between canyons, ridges, and the Frio and Nueces rivers draw motorcyclists like wildflowers attract honeybees. Sometimes the allure can be fatal. Since 2006, 10 motorcycle riders have lost their lives on the Twisted Sisters.

Traffic is especially heavy in November when the glowing big tooth maples at nearby Lost Maples State Natural Area bring crowds. In a good year, the fall color here is some of the best in Texas. The natural area gets about 70 percent of its visitors during the fall color season. To escape the leaf peepers, visit on a weekday during the spring or summer. In the state preserve, half a dozen hiking trails climb to scenic overlooks or meander along the spring-fed Sabinal River.

WILD RIDE

WHAT: Twisted Sisters

WHERE: Ranch Roads 337, 336, and 335 near Vanderpool. Lost Maples State Natural Area, 37221 FM 187, Vanderpool, TX; (830) 966-3413

COST: Lost Maples State Natural Area, $6 adults, 12 and under free.

PRO TIP: Lost Maples State Natural Area attracts big crowds in November when rare big tooth maples are in bloom. Admission is by reservation. For a more leisurely experience, plan your visit for a weekday in spring and summer when the nature preserve still has plenty of outdoor experiences to offer. For rates and reservations, visittexasstateparks.org, or call (512) 389-8900. For information only, call (800) 792-1112.

Left: *The natural area is a sanctuary for golden-cheeked warblers and other rare birds.*

Inset: *Lost Maples is a jumping off place for the winding Hill Country roads known as the Twisting Sisters.*

The natural area is home to abundant wildlife and birds, including rare black-capped vireos and golden-cheeked warblers.

If you don't have the time to drive the entire loop of the Twisted Sisters, which covers more than 100 miles, sample one of the most iconic drives, Ranch Road 337. The road twists and dips for 17 miles from Vanderpool to Leakey and continues on for another 21 miles to Camp Wood. It's a beautiful, scenic ride that many say is their favorite section of the Twisted Sisters. But with so much scenery to dazzle you, it's hard to pick a favorite.

High in the Hill Country, three corkscrew highways rollercoaster through more ups and downs than a high rise elevator.

FALL FOR THE FRIO

How can you escape the crowds at Garner State Park?

In the summer months, visitors smother Garner State Park with love. You can't blame them. They come to paddle and float the beautiful Frio River. They relax in the shade of towering cypress trees. They dance under the stars on an outdoor pavilion with an heirloom of a juke box that has been serenading two-steppers since the 1940s. On busy days, you need a reservation to get in the park, and the line at the gate can stretch for half a mile or more. But there's an easier way to do it: Visit in the off season and enjoy a hidden treasure of fall colors.

Hike up to the top of Old Baldy and take in the spectacular view of the Frio, outlined with the golden colors of ancient bald cypress trees. "In the off season, it's unbelievable how different this park is," says a member of the staff. "It's my favorite time of the year."

Big tooth maples, Spanish oaks, and red buds add their leaves to the autumn show. More than 16 miles of trails cross the angular terrain of the nearly 2,000-acre park. The first purchase of ranch land by conservationists in the 1930s might be the best $12 an acre any nature lover ever spent. That's how much it cost to buy the first 478 acres. The park is named for John Nance Garner, a rancher from nearby Uvalde who served as US vice president under Franklin D. Roosevelt. The Civilian Conservation Corps arrived in 1935 to construct many of the rock-hewn buildings the park still uses. The mess hall became the concession building that serves refreshments for the summer dances.

When you plan a visit to one of the busiest state parks in Texas, play it cool and come in the off-season.

Top left and right: *The less crowded off-season paints Garner State Park with fall color.*

Center left: *Campers enjoy the tranquility of the park.*

Bottom: *Birds sing the praises of the park's scenery.*

Photos courtesy of Texas Department of Parks and Wildlife

In the fall, nature supplies the music. You can hear it in the calls from some of the 200 species of birds that visit the park. It sounds in the melody of the Frio, rushing by over rocks. It's in the crackle of wood lighted in fireplaces that warm visitors in some of the park's cabins. Summer is nice, but the off-season is pretty special too. It's hard to imagine a better time to be here.

A LITTLE LESS CROWDED

WHAT: Garner State Park

WHERE: 234 Ranch Rd. 1059, Concan, TX

COST: $8 age 13 and up, 12 and under free. Reservations are needed, tpwd.texas.gov/state-parks/garner, or (830) 232-6132.

PRO TIP: Book one of the park's 13 cabins with fireplaces for $150 per night, two-night minimum. The cabins can sleep six. You have to bring your own blankets, sheets, pillows, dishes, and cookware. For reservations, visit texasstateparks.reserveamerica.com; or (512) 389-8900.

DANGEROUS DAYS AT THE STAR HOTEL

Why did a tombstone mark one of the resting places at this hotel?

There was a time when Lampasas was as rowdy as any town in the Hill Country. It was harassed by Indians, feuding cowboys,

and lethal gunfighters. One of its most infamous shootouts felled four state policemen at a local saloon. The shooters were later acquitted. But perhaps the most poignant victim of those wild days was a 15-year-old boy, waylaid by Indians. His tombstone stood outside the Star Hotel, a frontier stagecoach stop opened in 1853 and operated by his family. His name was James Edward Luther Gracy. The inscription on his stone, etched in the best attempt at spelling anyone could muster, read "killed & skelped by Indians."

Gracy and a neighbor boy were out looking for lost horses on foot on a fine spring April day in 1862 when they were suddenly surrounded by about 15 raiders on horseback. The other boy escaped and ran for help. Gracy wasn't so lucky. A rescue party found his body the

STOPPING TIME

WHAT: Keystone Star Hotel

WHERE: 404 E 2nd St., Lampasas, TX

COST: Free. The hotel is on private property, but it can be viewed from the street, where a historical marker tells of its colorful past.

PRO TIP: The nearby Keystone Square Museum, 303 S Western Ave., preserves the story of the town's early years. It opens from 10 a.m. to 4 p.m. Fridays and Saturdays. Admission is free; (512) 556-2224.

The grounds of this hotel once included a tombstone for a teenager "skelped by Indians."

Top: *The Star Hotel is restored as a private residence in Lampasas.*

Left inset: *In its heyday, the hotel boasted of steam heat.*

Right inset: *A marker remembers the son of the innkeepers who was killed by Indians.*

following morning and returned it to his parents, who buried him on the grounds of the hotel. Later, when Oak Hill Cemetery opened, his grave was relocated.

The Star Hotel grew into a sturdy, two-story structure, built of limestone. A new owner, J.R. Key, purchased it in 1926, added additional rooms, and renamed it the Keystone Hotel. In recent times, the hotel sat vacant until Austin resident Andrew Fish bought the landmark in 2017, and restored it. It is sometimes used for weddings and other special functions. Fish, an antique car collector, was originally looking for a building to house his car collection. He bought another nearby building to hold his extensive collection of vintage automobiles. The Limestone Hotel is one of the earliest landmarks in the Downtown Historic District. With the beautifully restored county courthouse, the district includes many buildings on the National Register of Historic Places.

STOP FOR PIE
AT THE APPLE STORE

Where can you find the apple capital of Texas?

It was a good day for apple pie lovers when Carol and Baxter Adams planted the first dwarf apple trees at their ranch in Medina in 1981. Love Creek Orchards became a favorite stop for travelers on the scenic Texas 16 drive between Kerrville and Bandera.

Medina grew to become the Apple Capital of Texas, sanctioned by the Texas legislature. *Texas Monthly* picked Love Creek's apple pie as one of the best in Texas. Under Bryan and Stacie Hutzler, who took over in 2007 after the Adamses retired, the Love Creek café still serves its famous apple pie. It takes five pounds of apples to make one. Love Creek produces more than 50 other items, made from apples, from jams and jellies to ice cream. Old-fashioned apple butter, made from a secret recipe, is one of the top sellers.

APPLE CAPITAL

WHAT: Love Creek Orchards Store and Café

WHERE: 14024 Texas 16 N, Medina, TX

COST: $32.99 for the Grand Champion Apple Pie, made with five pounds of apples.

PRO TIP: Try the spicy pepper jack burger ($11.25) at the café, with a slice of apple pie topped with apple ice cream for dessert. It is open for lunch weekdays (except Wednesdays) and on Saturday and Sunday. The store ships pies, jams, jellies, apple butter, and other items; lovecreekorchards.com or (830) 200-0302.

Fall is a popular season to visit. The apple orchards are in recovery from the devastating 2021 freeze, but bigtooth maples dot the nearby hills and Lost Maples State Natural Area is nearby. Love Creek also hosts a popular pumpkin patch celebration each October. Refreshments include fresh-made apple cider.

Top: *The Apple Store features foods made from Medina's favorite fruit.*

Inset: *You can purchase an apple pie in a jar ready to be baked.*

Apple trees aren't the only improvement the Adamses gave the local landscape. They also gifted part of their ranch to the Nature Conservancy. It became the basis for the 2,508-acre Love Creek Preserve. The pristine sanctuary, watered with many springs and protected by tall cliffs, protects more than two miles of Honey Creek. It is periodically open for guided tours by reservation; (210) 224-8774.

In the tiny town of Medina, apples don't fall too far from the treats, which include delicious apple pie.

ENCORE AT TAPATIO SPRINGS

What resort has the King of Country Music singing its praises?

It's not oceanfront property, but it'll do. Nestled in the scenic limestone hills near Boerne, Tapatio Springs Resort got a new lease on life when country superstar George Strait and his longtime business partner Tom Cusick bought it out of bankruptcy in 2011. The two played golf there often. They hated to see the once carefully-tended resort slip into disrepair. They began renovations, but the biggest part of the makeover wasn't finished until 2019 after a fire destroyed the clubhouse.

Centerpiece of the new work is a glass-walled, 47,000-square-feet clubhouse, where La Cascada Bar & Grill overlooks the rolling terrain of the golf course. You might see George strolling by after a round. An avid golfer, he hosts the Vaqueros del Mar Invitational charity golf tournament each October. It's a private event, but you're welcome to bunk in George's room, when he isn't using it. The two-bedroom George Strait Suite is the largest of the resort's 111 rooms. It features two fireplaces. Decorations include framed hit records and posters from concerts and George's only movie, *Pure Country*. Rates start at $800 per night.

MAKE YOURSELF AT HOME

WHAT: Tapatio Springs Hill Country Resort

WHERE: 1 Resort Way, Boerne, TX

COST: Weekday room rates start at $135; tapatiosprings.com or 1-888-299-7485.

PRO TIP: La Cascada hosts singer-songwriter concerts on Friday and Saturday nights featuring regional artists. George has been known to drop in too.

Top left: *A cascade of water adds beauty to the golf course.*

Top right: *Tapatio Springs was given a new lease on life by its owner country music legend George Strait.*

Bottom left: *Warm your feet by the fire pit.*

Bottom right: *George Strait brought Tapatio Springs back to prominence.*

Or just kick back and relax on the spacious 220-acre grounds. Order a shot of George's Codigo 1530 brand of tequila. Raise a toast to the work that breathed new life into a faded resort. It's one of the best encores the King of Country music ever made. Maybe he'll write a song about it.

Once loved, Tapatio Springs was slowly fading into the sunset, until George Strait found the music in it.

WHEN TEXAS WAS A GARDEN OF EDEN

Was the bravest man on the Texas frontier a botanist?

Maybe so. There is no record of Ferdinand Lindheimer ever showing fear. The Hill Country was a dangerous wilderness when he roamed it with a horse-drawn, two-wheeled cart. He wasn't concerned about Comanches or any other marauding bands of Native Americans. The blue-eyed explorer with a bushy black beard was too focused on plants. He collected and identified hundreds of them. He shipped them off to form new Texas collections at Harvard, the Smithsonian Institution, the Royal Botanical Gardens at Krew, and other renowned places of learning. And some he brought back to plant in the gardens of the house he built on the banks of the Comal River in New Braunfels. The modest four-room house is preserved as a museum operated by the New Braunfels Conservation Society.

HOUSE AND GARDEN

WHAT: Ferdinand Lindheimer House Museum

WHERE: 491 Comal Ave., New Braunfels, TX

COST: Tours are given by request by the New Braunfels Conservation Society. Prices vary. For information, call (830) 629-2943.

PRO TIP: If you can't be there for a tour, the house and gardens can be viewed from the outside. A large downtown mural depicts Lindheimer on one of his plant-gathering journeys.

Native Americans allowed a brave scientist to roam freely across the Hill Country, collecting the plants that made him the father of Texas botany.

Top left: *Lindheimer braved the wilds of the frontier.*

Top right: *The house of Ferdinand Lindheimer, known as the father of Texas botany, is preserved in New Braunfels.*

Bottom: *Lindheimer's Silktassel and more than 60 other plants are named in his honor.*

Lindheimer lived enough adventures to fill 10 lifetimes. He was a soldier, scout, newspaper editor, and teacher. He was the guide who brought the first German settlers to New Braunfels, picking out the location for the future town where the Comal River joined the Guadalupe. He told Prince Carl of Solms-Braunfels, "I could lead you to more fertile soil, but not to purer water."

The house where he lived with his wife and four children displays some of the many plants he collected. More than 60 are named in his honor, including some as well known as prickly pear cactus, opuntia lindheimeri. Lindheimer was able to travel unmolested among the Indians during his years of collecting on the frontier. Some speculate the natives may have regarded him as a medicine man since he kept gathering so many plants—which they also prized. He sometimes traveled with the Comanches. He became friends with the war chief Santana.

Settlers in New Braunfels held him in high regard too. Lindheimer was picked to be the first editor of the *Neu Braunfelser Zeitung*, the state's longest-running German-language newspaper. He held that post from 1852 to 1872.

DINE IN A MOVIE SET

Did the pretty house that holds a pleasant café in Kingsland once serve meals to cannibals?

Only in the movies. There's nothing very scary about having a delicious steak at the Grand Central Café in Kingsland, but if you know the history of the house it's in, it might make the hair stand up on the back of your neck. Once it was home to a family of cannibals when it was the main location for *The Texas Chainsaw Massacre*.

The house originally sat at the end of a lonely lane in Round Rock when it was a not so home sweet home for Leatherface and the rest of his demented family in the 1973 horror film classic. Despite its star status, the house sat vacant and deteriorating for several years after the film was released. Ironically, the house that featured chainsaw slashings wound up being cut into pieces itself.

It was purchased in 1998 by the owners of the Antlers Inn and disassembled to make the move to its new home in Kingsland. Now handsomely restored, it's a popular restaurant next door to the historic hotel. The hotel opened in 1901 and in the early days it served railroad travelers who came by excursion trains from Austin, Houston, and other cities. The Austin and

CURTAIN CALL

WHAT: Grand Central Café

WHERE: 1010 King Court, Kingsland, TX

COST: At dinner, steak Oscar topped with lump crab, is $27. The café serves breakfast until 2 p.m. It opens for breakfast and lunch Wednesday–Sunday, and dinner, Wednesday–Saturday; kingslandgrandcentraol.com or 1-800-383-0007.

PRO TIP: Accommodations at the Antlers Inn range from vintage hotel rooms to two-room cabins and cottages; info@theantlers.com or 1-800-383-0007.

Top: *The building that houses the Grand Central Café starred in* The Texas Chainsaw Massacre *before it became a popular restaurant.*

Inset: *Memorabilia from the movie decorates the bar.*

Northwestern Railroad built a nearby depot. By the 1950s, the hotel enjoyed a location close to the newly dammed Lake Granite Shoals, now Lake LBJ.

The graceful Victorian house of the Grand Central Café compliments the tranquil setting. It's not scary anymore, but it's still a perfect place for a getaway.

The Grand Central Café may look familiar to fans of a classic horror movie.

SOURCES

Sweet Scent: Moore, Chrissy. "One Man's Road to Herbal Success: An Interview." April 26, 2021. The Herb Society of America Blog. herbsocietyblog.wordpress.com/2021/04/26/one-mans-road-to-herbal-success-an-interview. urbanherbal.com

Spirits Haunt the Backbone Tavern: Wallace, Christian. "The Best Honky Tonks in Texas," Sept. 2019, *Texas Monthly*. Seymour, Corey. "Best Old Time Honky Tonk in Texas," Nov. 2019, *Vogue. Unsolved Mysteries*, Feb. 22, 2017

Swine Dive: Reeves, Kimberly. "Last Goodbye to Aquarena Springs," Nov. 14, 2008, *The Austin Chronicle*, austinchronicle.com/news/2008-11-14; meadowscenter.txstate.edu/education/glass-bottomboats.html

Hidden Treasure around the Bend: Garner, Chett. "Gorman Falls: The Most Beautiful Waterfall in Texas," *The Daytripper*, Oct. 12, 2019, thedaytripper.com. Thomas, Les. "Beauty at the Bend," *Southern Living Magazine*, March 2003, southernliving.com/travel/southwest/beauty-at-the-bend

Flower Power: Sokolove, Sofia. "Sowing Seeds," *Texas Highways Magazine*, October 1, 2014. Lewis, Sallie. "Wildflower Man," *Texas Parks & Wildlife Magazine*, April, 2016. "John R. Thomas '70," Sam Houston State University Office of Alumni Relations, Distinguished Alumni Banquet, Oct. 18, 1991, shsu.edu/dept/office-of-alumni-rlations/awards/distinguished/people/thomas.html

Gruene Hall's Ace in the Hole: Scudder, Charles. "Inside George Strait's private, surprise show at historic Gruene Hall," Nov. 17, 2016, Dallas Morning News. gruenehall.com

Long, Strange Voyage to Texas: Pearlharbor.org. "The Fate of the Captured Midget Submarine HA. 19," Sept. 7, 2018. Archeology, The Submarines, archaeology.org/exclusive/articles/5056-pearl-harbor-archaeology-the-submarines

Better Mileage than a Mule: Heller, Chris. "Whatever Happened to the Wild Camels of the American West," *Smithsonian Magazine*, Aug. 6, 2015. campverdegeneralstore.com/main/history

Clovis Has Left the Building: Scudder, Charles. "Dim the lights: Number of Texas dance halls is dwindling, but some keep two-stepping," Dec. 22, 2015, Dallas Morning News, Lehmann, Herman. *Nine Years Among the Indians, 1870-1879, The Story of the Captivity*

and Life of a Texan Among the Indians, University of New Mexico Press, 1993. *Cherry Springs Dance Hall, the Handbook of Texas*. Texas Dance Hall Preservation, Inc., texasdancehall.org

A Bakery Rises to the Top: naegelins.com/about. Greene, Daniel P. "New Braunfels, TX." Sept. 24, 2020. tshaonline.org/handbook/entries/new-braunfels-tx. Lawrence, Katie. "Sink Your Teeth into Authentic German Strudel at Naegelin's, the Oldest Bakery in Texas." June 3, 2020. onlyinyourstate.com/texas/oldest-bakery-tx

Snail Mail Survives at Hye: Barr, Michael. "Looking Back at Hye Society." March 14, 2016. texasescapes.com/michaelbarr/hye-society.htm. Bruin, Richard. "Hye, TX." Feb. 1, 1995. tshaonline.org/handbook/entries/hye-tx. MacCormack, Zeke. "Hye Residents Mobilize to Save Post Office." Aug. 22, 2011. My SA. mysanantonio.com/news/local_news/article/hye-residents-mobilize-to-save-post-office-2117351.php

A Feisty Fowl: Michael Barr. "All's Well at Castell's General Store Near Llano." Aug. 8, 2017. *Texas Highways*. texashighways.com/travel/all-is-well-at-castells-general-store. Holley, Joe. "Castell Retains Hill Country's Rural Charm." April 10, 2015. *Houston Chronicle*. houstonchronicle.com/news/columnists/native-texan/article/houston-news-6191930.php. Stellfox, Marcy. "Five Reasons You Need to Kick Back in Castell." July 22, 2016. texashillcountry.com/visit-castell

Rock of Ages: "Enchanted Rock State Natural Area." tpwd.texas.gov/state-parks/enchanted-rock/park_history. Makepeace, Caroline. "Tips for Climbing Enchanted Rock Texas—A Spiritual Place." Jan. 30, 2013. ytravelblog.com/enchanted-rock-texas. Robertson, Katelyn. "The Hauntings of Enchanted Rock." Nov. 13, 2016. texashillcountry.com/hauntings-enchanted-rock

Cruising the Canyon: vtrc.com/cruises. lakesandhills.com/eagles.htm. Freeman, Suzanne. "Bald Eagles Join Other Winter Texans." Oct. 26, 2020. 101highlandlakes.com/news/bald-eagles-in-the-highland-lakes. highlandlakesofburnetcounty.com/american-eagles-winter-in-burnet-county

Ancient Oil: texashillcountryoliveco.com. italicaoliveoil.com/facts-about-olive-oil. Ghose, Tia. "The Origins of the Olive Tree Revealed," Feb. 5, 2013. livescience.com/26887-olive-tree-origins.html

Burgers Fit for a King: Gentile, Dan. "The Best Road Trip Food Stops." foodnetwork.com/restaurants/photos/best-road-trip-food. Lawrence, Katie. "This Tiny Drive In May Just Be the Best Kept Secret in Texas." July 17, 2018. onlyinyourstate.

com/texas/tiny-drive-in-tx. McLeod, Gerald E. "Day Trips." July 19, 2002. *The Austin Chronicle.* austinchronicle.com/columns/2002-07-19/97571. stormsrestaurants.com

Surely You're Jousting: Barguairena, Edgar. "3 Gorgeous Hill Country Castles Near Austin." Jan. 6, 2015. The Austinot. austinot.com/texas-hill-country-castles. Regulski, Elisa. "Entering this Hidden Castle near Austin Will Make You Feel Like You're in Fairy Tale." September 8, 2016. onlyinyourstate.com/texas/austin/hill-country-castle-austin. spacesift.com/listing/falkenstein-castle-event-rental-austin-tx

The Town the Map Forgot: roadsideamerica.com/tip/1288. Monk, Matthew. "5 Things You Didn't Know About Oatmeal, Texas." June 16, 2013. texashillcountry.com/oatmeal-texas-things-you-didnt-know. "Oatmeal 44 Festival." oatmealfestival.org/history

Historic Hardware: Historic Walking Tour (Henne Hardware). July 24, 2020. youyube.com. Goff, Myra Lee Adams. "Henne Hardware Survives 148 Years Downtown." Nov. 2, 2014. Sophienburg Museum and Archives. sophienburg.com/henne-hardware-survives-148-years-downtown. Klein, Kate. "More than 160 Years of History at Henne Hardware."June 29, 2018. hardwareretailing.com/160-years-history-henne-hardware

Boots on Parade: Courtney, David. "The Texanist." Nov. 2015. texasmonthly.com/the-culture/the-texanist-on-the-pronunciation-of-pecan. Cox, Mike. "Texas Tales." Jan. 16, 2019. texasescapes.com/mikecoxtexastales/boots-on-fence-posts.htm. Hughes, Martha and Ronnie. "Why Do Texans Place Old Boots on Fence Posts?" Sept. 20, 2021. rvcrossroads.com/tag/why-do-texans-place-old-boots-on-fence-posts. "One Dusty Track." 1dustytrack.blogspot.com/2018/12/postcard-from-boot-hill-texas.html

Grape Expectations: "Celebrate Grape Stomp Like a Pro in Fredericksburg." July 16, 2021. visitfredericksburgtx.com/blog/post/celebrate-grape-stomp-like-a-pro. Cope, Jeff. "Grape Stomping in Texas 2021." July 16, 2021. *Texas Wine Lover.* txwinelover.com/2021/07/grape-stomping-in-texas-2021. Wilcox, Kathleen. "Grape Stomping is a Photogenic Process with Practical Benefits." March 17, 2020. *Wine Enthusiast.* winemag.com/2020/03/17/stomping-grapes-winemaking-crush

World Class Spur: atlasobscura.com/places/worlds-largest-spur. waylandthesmith.com/about. guinnessworldrecords.com/world-records/largest-spur. "World's Biggest Spur." Sept. 12, 2016. talesfromthewayside.com/blog-1/2016/9/10/giant-metal-spur-wayside-oddities

A Sleeping Giant: lakesandhills.com/buchanan%20dam/index.htm. hillcountryportal.com/buchanandam.html. lcra.org/water/dams-and-lakes. highlandlakesofburnetcounty.com/american-eagles-winter-in-burnet-county. Interview with Steve Buchanan of the Visitor Center, conducted Aug. 12, 2021

Don't Get Sidetracked; Take the Hill Country Flyer: austinsteamtrain.org/make-reservations/termsconditions. McPike, Kristen. "Cotton, Cattle, and Railroads." texasourtexas.texaspbs.org/the-eras-of-texas/cotton-cattle-railroads

The Dog Who Lived Forever: mason.ploud.net/old-yeller-day. Lackey, Dee. "Mason's Master Storyteller Still Enchanting Readers." *Authentic Texas.* authentictexas.com/master-mason-storyteller-fred-gipson-still-enchanting-readers

Anchors Away on Main Street: Nimitz Hotel Records, 1847-1905, Briscoe Center For American History, The University of Texas at Austin. Nimitz Hotel, Handbook of Texas, Texas State Historical Association

Magic on the River Road: Water-Oriented Recreation District of Comal County, wordcc.com. actionangler.net

A Blind Man with Remarkable Vision: Hallowell, John. "Blind Man With a Vision," Aug. 9, 2018, Highland Lakes Weekly. Johnson, Adam Rankin (1834-1922), Handbook of Texas, Texas State Historical Association

Busy Bees: McCleod, Gerald E., "Day Trips Llano's Fain's Honey Company and Fredericksburg's Pedernales Brewing Company meet in a bar, and the results will surprise you," Oct. 3, 2014, *The Austin Chronicle.* fainshoney.com

Forgotten Peacemaker: Handbook of Texas, tsaonline.org/handbook/entries/Katemcy-tx. Barr, Michael. Hindsights column, "Looking back at: Katemcy-No Town Without a Post Office," Jan. 30, 2019, texasescapes.com

Healing Waters: lampasas.org/396/historic-hostess-house. "Springs Rooted in Lampasas History," *Fort Hood Sentinel,* Dec. 22, 2015. Simek, Peter. "5 Magical Natural Springs in Texas," *Texas Heritage for Living,* Aug. 26, 219; texasheritageforliving.com/ 5-magical-springs-in-texas

Happy Hour at the P.O.: fischerstore.com/history.html. Barr, Michael. Hindsights Column, "Looking back at: Fischer Store—Prime Real Estate," June 14, 2019, texasescapes.com

Texas-Sized Christmas Ornament: Lewis, Sallie. "Beyond Oktoberfest: Meet Fredericksburg's Lesser Known Traditions," *Texas Highways Magazine*, May 7, 2021. VisitFredericksburg.com/blog/post/the-fredericksburg-german-christmas-pyramid

A Trip to Blanco Makes Scents: "Lavender Sales Are Surging Amid Pandemic," Aug. 20, 2020, *Southern Living Magazine*

Whopper of a Fish Story: Hanna Springs Sculpture Garden, Lampasas Association for the Arts, lafta.org/sculpture-garden.html

Treasure for the Taking: Barr, Michael. "Looking back at The Lost Spanish Mine," *Texas Escapes*, Feb. 1, 2017, texasescapes.com/michaelbarr/lost-spanish-mine.htm. Dobie, J. Frank. Coronado's Children, The Literary Guild of New York, 1931

A Day Made for a Sunday House: "American Architectural Oddities The Sunday Houses of Fredericksburg, TX, June 28, 2021. "Sunday Houses," Handbook of Texas, tshaonline.org/handbook/entries/sunday-houses

A Fort Filled with Future Generals: "Fort Mason," Handbook of Texas, Texas State Historical Association. "Robert E. Lee in Texas," sonofthesouth.net/leefoundation/lee_in_texas.htm. "Mason: Fort Mason," Texas Forts Trail Region, texasfortstrail.com/plain-your-adventure/historic-sites-and-cities/sites/fort-mason

High Price for Comfort: "Treue Der Union Monument Represents an Incredible Cost For Comfort," Texas Public Radio, May 24, 2018; tpr.org/arts-culture/2018-05-24/treue-der-union-monument-represents-an-incredible-cost-for-comfort

Disappearing Mountain: Henderson, Jim. "Color of Capitol's granite puts legend in question," March 9, 2003, *Houston Chronicle*. Freeman, Suzanne. "Rocky Histories: Granite Mountain Chipping Away," Nov. 5, 2019, *Picayune Magazine*

Quiet Please, Cattle Drive Passing through: thewittliffcollections.txstate.edu/exhibitions/Treasures-of-the-Wittliff.html. Leydon, Joe. "The Wittliff Collections," *Cowboys and Indians Magazine*, Jan. 1. 2015

Ride the Wild Chute: Nbtexas.org/2579/Comal-River-info. "Comal River," Handbook of Texas, June 23, 2020, tshaonline.org/handbook

Nutty and Nice: Thomas, Les. "Gifts in a Nutshell," Nov. 2008, *Southern Living Magazine*.

McCleod, Gerald E. "Day Trips: Millican Pecan Company, San Saba," Oct. 2, 2020, *The Austin Chronicle*

Monumental Move: Harrison, Conor. "Stonehenge II begins journey to new home," *Kerrville Daily Times*, Aug. 10, 2010. Hill Country Arts Foundation, "Stonehenge II," hcaf.com/stonehenge-ii

Finding Miracles in Utopia: Home, Justin. "Unique Texas towns: How Utopia, Comfort got their names," KSAT.com, Nov. 28, 2019. Wheeler, Camille. "Vanderpool to Utopia," *Texas Co-op Magazine*, Nov. 2008, texascooppower.com/travel/central-texas/vanderpool-to-utopia. Handbook of Texas, tshaonline.org/handbook/entries/utopia-tx." Utopia Texas, "An Ideally, Perfect Place" utopiatexas.info/about.html

Secret Swimming Hole: krausesprings.net. austintexas.org/listings/krause-springs/4786

Llano Rocks: Ostdick, John. "Rock Heaven," April, 2018, *Texas Parks & Wildlife Magazine*. Weisman, Dale. "Small-Town Business Spotlight: Collectors Roll to Enchanted Rocks in Llano for Geological Rarities," Aug. 2020, *Texas Highways Magazine*

Lodge in a Landmark: "Landmark Inn State Historic Site," Handbook of Texas. Landmark Inn State Historic Site, Texas Historical Commission, thc.texas/gov/historic-sites/landmark-inn/bed-and-breakfast

On This Campus, a River Runs through It: txstate.edu>about>history>traditions/old-fish-hatchery-ponds.html

Saved by a Hair: Hagerty, Kyle. "Barbershops Are Back And Bucking Retail Trends," July 6, 2017, Forbes. newbraunfelsconservation.org/buckhorn-barbershop-museum

Some Small Wonders in Luckenbach: Patterson, Becky Crouch. Hondo My Father, Shoal Creek Publishers, Inc., 1979, "Luckenbach Daylight," pages 210-212

Stay a Night on Teddy's Train: 6666ranch.com/about-burnett-family. fredericksburgescapes.com/vacation-rentals/pullman-train-car

The Captain's Mansion: "A Rich History," yoschreiner.com/pages/history. Schreiner, Charles Armand (1838-1927), Handbook of Texas. Haley, J. Evetts. Charles Schreiner, General Merchandise, Texas State Historical Association, 1944

The Hill Country's Best Old Curiosity Stop: bandracoboycapital.com/business/frontier-times-museum; frontiertimesmagazine.com;

"LCRA Bandera Electric Co-op award $6,596 grant to Frontier Times Museum," lcra.org/news/news-releases/lcra-bandera-electric-co-op-award-6596-grant-to-frontier-times-museum

This Old House Crossed the Ocean: Simek, Peter. "City Spotlight: Castroville," *Texas Heritage for Living*, texasheritageforliving.com/texas-travel/city-spotlght-castroville-texas. steinbachhouse.org

The Hole of No Return: Texas Co-Op Power, "Dark Landmark," April 2020. Texas State Historical Association Handbook of Texas, tshaonline.org/handbook/entries/dead-mans-hole

Saving the Show: Blackburn, Robin, "Brauntex Marking 75 Years," Jan. 4, 2017, *New Braunfels Herald-Zeitung*. brauntex.org

Honky-Tonk Man: Quine, Katy. "What is a Honky-Tonk?" Grand Ole Opry, opry.com/story/what-is-a-honky-tonk: Wallace, Christian. "The Best Honky-Tonks in Texas," Sept., 2019, *Texas Monthly*. "Arkey Blue," Frontier Times Museum, frontiertimesmuseum.org/arkeyblue.html

Secrets of the Deep: Bond, Louis. "The Fatal Allure of Jaco's Well," 2001, visitwimberley.com/jacobswell/lbond/index.shtml. "Jacob's Well institutes admission fee, new rules," KXAN, March 30, 2015; hayscountytx.com/departments/hays-county-parks-recreation/jacobs-well-natural-area

Stopping Time at the Five and Dime: Smith-Rodgers, Cheryl. "Five-and-Dime Happy Times," Feb. 2011, *Texas Coop Power Magazine*, texascooppower.com/texas-stories/history/five-and-dime-happy-times

Tunnel Vision: Texas Parks and Wildlife Department; texasstateparks.org

Guest Who?: Cox, Mike. "Lincoln Slept here." July 26, 2014. Texas Tales. texasescapes.com/mikecoxtexastales/lincoln-slept-here.htm. Goff, Myra Lee Adams. "The Queen and Princess of Buildings Around Main Plaza." Dec. 14, 2014. Sophienburg Museum and Archives. sophienburg.com/the-queen-and-princess-of-buildings-around-main-plaza

Sunsets at the Stonewall: Egan, John. "New York Times Checks in with Big Praise for Hip Hill Country Motel." Sept. 26, 2021. Culture Map. sanantonio.culturemap.com/news/travel/07-26-21-inew-york-timesi-checks-in-with-praise-for-central-texas-motel-owners-sa. Price, Pamela. "Stonewall Motor Lodge Will Bridge Past, Present." The Texas Wildflower. thetexaswildflower.com/stonewall-motor-lodge-motel-texas-lbj. stonewallmotorlodge.com/our-story

Avoid the Redhead: "Nine Pin Bowling." en.wikipedia.org/wiki/Nine-pin_bowling. Knapp, Deborah. "Texas Niners: the Last Bastion of Nine Pin Bowling Lives on in San Antonio." Aug. 25, 2018. KENS5 TV. kens5.com/article/news/texas-niners-the-last-bastion-of-nine-pin-bowling-lives-on-in-san-antonio/273-587471515. LeCompte, Mary Lou. "Nine pin Bowling." tshaonline.org/handbook/entries/ninepin-bowling. Patoski, Joe Nick. "Still Standing After all These Years." May 2009. Texas Coop Power Newsletter. texascooppower.com/texas-stories/life-arts/still-standing-after-all-these-years

Stollen Goods?: McCulolough, Bob. "A Taste of Alsace." Feb. 1, 2014. *Texas Highways*. texashighways.com/eat-drink/a-taste-of-alsace. habysbakery.com

Magical Medina: Silva, Jourdan. "You can Float Down the Most Beautiful Hidden River Near San Antonio This Summer." Narcity. April 26, 2019. narcity.com/san-antonio/the-medina-river-in-bandera-texas-is-the-perfect-tubing-spot. Wendlandt, Catherine. "Float the Medina River." *Houstonia Magazine*. Nov. 6, 2020. houstoniamag.com/travel-and-outdoors/float-the-medina-river

Diamonds in the Stream: roadsideamerica.com/tip/72488. Berry, Kaitlin. "Kerrville Main Street to Hold Dedication Ceremony for Guadalupe Bass Public Art Project." Jan. 20, 2017. kerrvilletx.gov/documentcenter/view/30846/kerrville-main-street-to-hold-dedication-ceremony-for-guadalupe-bass-public-art-proj?bidid=. Prout, Tammy. "'Lupe' Finds a Home in Kerrville." Feb. 9, 2017. Hill Country Community Journal. hccommunityjournal.com/article_dc38471c-ed5c-11e6-ad37-07a348671c74.html

Curtain Up: Merhar, Judy Rae. "Restored Globe Theater Preserves Old Pastime in Bertram, Texas." Jan. 27, 2017. *The Austinot*. austinot.com/globe-theatre-bertram-texas globetheatretx.com/history.htm

Food of the Gods: Iseman, Courtney. "Everything You've Ever Wanted to Know about Mead." Aug. 15, 2019. delish.com/food/a28691670/what-is-mead-honey-wine. "The Surprising Meaning of Honeymoon Explained." dictionary.com/e/honeymoon. bluelotuswinery.com/texas-mead-works. Taylor, Elise. "Why the World's Oldest Drink Is on the Rise Again." Nov. 15, 2018. *Vogue*. vogue.com/article/why-mead-is-popular-again

Heading for a Hundred: cridersrandd.com. kerrvilletexascvb.com/business/criders-rodeo-dancehall. Brand, Heather. "Crider's Is Still Riding And Dancing Along the Guadalupe River in Hunt." July 28, 2020. *Texas Highways*. texashighways.com/travel-news/small-town-business-spotlight-criders-outdoor-rodeo-and-dance-guadalupe-hunt

Music and a Meal: Honky Tonk Foodie. "Find Freiheit Country Store for Delicious Surprises." Sept. 26, 2019. texashillcountry.com/find-freiheit-country-store-surprises. freiheitcountrystore.net. Nelson, Rachel. "Freiheit Country Store: Eatery Serves Food, Live Tunes." Jan. 28, 2018. Community Impact Newspaper. communityimpact.com/austin/new-braunfels/dining/2018/01/22/freiheit-country-store-eatery-serves-food-live-tunes

Celebrated Cukes: Nalewicki, Jennifer. "These Pickles Are Worth Relishing." Feb. 1, 2014. *Texas Highways*. texashighways.com/eat-drink/pickles-worth-relishing. ficklepickles.com/category/from-the-jar

Massacre of a Wagon Train: Martha Virginia Webster Strickland Simmons Narrative, 1912, Briscoe Center for American History, the University of Texas at Austin. Clifton, Daniel. "On the road to history: Stickling, Texas," July 27, 2018, 101highlandlakes.com/news/the-history-of-strickling-texas

A Road Runs through It: jonesaroundtheworld.com/quotes-about-texas. "Hunt, Texas." texashillcountry.com/hunt-texas. Reynolds, Virginia. "This One Time at Summer Camp." *Paper City*. papercitymag.com/culture/texas-best-summer-camps-mystic-waldemer-vista. "Rides and Drives." backroadstexas.net/rides-and-drives. Wiley, Tom. "TX 39 Near Kerrville." Oct. 2, 2015. Ride Texas. ridetexas.com/tx-39-near-kerrville

A Bison Found and a Waterfall Lost: Osborn, Claire. "700-year-old bison on display at Burnet County Museum," Sept. 25, 2018, Austin American-Statesman. fallsmuseum.org

Built to Last: Giles, Alfred (1853-1920), Handbook of Texas, Texas State Historical Association. Moon, Bryden. "Kendall County Connection to Alamo Plaza," Echoes...from the Archives," The Dietert Historical Archives, Patrick Heath Public Library, ci.boerne.tx.us. Barr, Michael. Hindsights column, "Looking Back at Alfred Giles, Texas Architect," June 1, 2016, texasescapes.com/michaelbarr/alfred-giles-texas-architect.htm

High on Pie!: Lawrence, Katie. "A Tiny Shop in Texas, The Blue Bonnet Cafe Serves Mouth Watering Pie." June 20, 2020. onlyinyourstate.com/texas/tiny-shop-pie-tx. O'Leary, Joanne. "Blue Bonnet Cafe Named Best 'Hole in the Wall' Diner in Texas." March 9, 2021. Chron. chron.com/food/article/best-diner-hole-in-wall-blue-bonnet-cafe-food-16011964.php. Ramsey, Sarah. "The Blue Bonnet Cafe is a Texas Institution." July 2, 2020. wideopeneats.com/blue-bonnet-cafe

Gems for the Picking: Kissko, Brenda. "Hunting Topaz," May, 2020, *Texas Coop Power Magazine*. Mason Country Collectibles, masoncountrycollectibles.com

Say Hello to the Twisted Sisters: Wheeler, Camille, "Vanderpool to Utopia Soak up the spectacular scenery...and keep both hands on the wheel," Nov., 2008, *Texas Coop Power*, texascooppower.com/travel/central-texas/vanderpool-to-utopia. Locke, Russ, "Twisted Sisters: The Texas Hill Country's Most Famous Trio," July 8, 2013, *Rider Magazine*, ridermagazine.com/2013/07/08/twisted-sisters-the-texas-hill-countrys-most-famous-trio

Fall for the Frio: "Must-See Fall Foliage Spots in Texas," Sept. 2017, *Texas Highways Magazine*. "Garner State Park," Handbook of Texas, Texas State Historical Association

Dangerous Days at the Star Hotel: Radcliff, Kris. "Keystone Hotel Renovations Wrap Up" kcentv.com/article/news/local/lampasas-keystone-hotel-continues-renovation-project/500-4b3c65f3-91d2-4792-8076-3c20f5da799f

Stop for Pie at the Apple Store: McLeod, Gerald E. "Love Creek Orchards has the only tree-ripe apples available in the U.S. in early July," July 13, 2012, *The Austin Chronicle*

Encore at Tapatio Springs: Perez, Mellanie. "Two Years After Fire, George Strait's Tapatio Springs Back to 'Having a Good Time,'" Dec. 11, 2019, *Texas Highways Magazine*. tapatiosprings.com

When Texas Was a Garden of Eden: Cortez, Dyanne Fry. "The Plant Gatherer," *Texas Parks & Wildlife Magazine*, Jan./Feb. 2013

Dine in a Movie Set: "Grand Central Café," kingslandgrandcentral.com/about-the-chainsaw-house. Bloom, John. "They Came, They Sawed," Nov. 2004, *Texas Monthly*

INDEX